LINGUISTICS

Jean Aitchison is a Senior Lecturer in Linguistics at the University of London, though she has also lectured widely in other parts of the world, including the USA, India and various European countries. She is convinced that an understanding of language is an enormous help in solving many human problems, and is determined to spread a knowledge of linguistics to a wider, non-university audience. She is the author of *The Articulate Mammal: An Introduction to Psycholinguistics* (2nd edition 1983), *Language Change: Progress or Decay* (1981) and *Words in the Mind: An Introduction to the Mental Lexicon* (1987).

D0167909

TEACH YOURSELF BOOKS

LINGUISTICS

Jean Aitchison

Senior Lecturer in Linguistics
London School of Economics

TEACH YOURSELF BOOKS

Hodder and Stoughton

First printed under the title 'General Linguistics' 1972
Second edition 1978
Third edition 1987

British Library Cataloguing in Publication Data
Aitchison, Jean
Linguistics.—3rd ed.—(Teach yourself
books).
1. Linguistics
I. Title   II. Series
410   P121

ISBN 0 340 41764 1

Printed in Great Britain for
Hodder and Stoughton Educational
a division of Hodder and Stoughton Ltd,
Mill Road, Dunton Green, Sevenoaks, Kent,
by Richard Clay Ltd, Bungay, Suffolk
Photosêt by Rowland Phototypesetting Ltd,
Bury St Edmunds, Suffolk

Contents

Preface   7

PART ONE   **Starting Out**
  1   What is Linguistics?   11
  2   What is Language?   19
  3   The Study of Language   29
  4   Deciding Where to Begin   36

PART TWO   **The Inner Circles**
  5   Sound Patterns   45
  6   Words and Pieces of Words   56
  7   Sentence Patterns   68
  8   Meaning   84

PART THREE   **The Outer Rings**
  9   Using Language   97
  10   Language and Society   105
  11   Language and Mind   119

PART FOUR   **Changes and Comparisons**
  12   Language Change   131
  13   Comparing Languages   142

PART FIVE   **Towards a Universal Grammar**
  14   Seeking a Suitable Framework   157
  15   Trouble with Transformations   171
  16   The New-look Grammar   182

Suggestions for Further Reading   193
List of Symbols and Abbreviations   199
Index   203

Preface

This book is an introduction to introductions to linguistics.

There are several books on the market which call themselves 'introductions' to the subject, but which are in fact more suited to second-year students.

This book is to help people working by themselves to break into the 'charmed circle' of linguistics. It explains basic concepts and essential terminology.

It is not a bedside reading book, and contains no chatty anecdotes. It is a straightforward handbook for those who wish to know about the subject. Linguistics is a highly technical field, and technical vocabulary cannot be avoided.

Linguistics is a field torn apart by controversies. Wherever possible, I have taken a 'middle-of-the-road' view. Not that a middle-of-the-road view is necessarily right, but it is possibly more helpful for those new to the subject. Hopefully, readers will view this book as a stepping-stone to some of the works suggested for further reading (p. 193), and will eventually decide for themselves on which side of the road they wish to stand over current linguistics issues.

Linguistics is a fast-changing subject, and parts of it have moved on considerably since the first (1972) and second (1978) editions of this book were published. This edition preserves around two-thirds of the previous version. The remainder has either been drastically altered, or is completely new. In particular, there are three new chapters dealing with topics which have come to the forefront in recent years: the use of language in ways which cannot be predicted from the linguistic structure (pragmatics), different language types (linguistic typology), and Chomsky's latest attempt to specify universal features underlying human language ('Government and Binding' theory).

I am most grateful to all those who have made helpful suggestions and comments—in particular John Ayto of London, Keith Brown of the University of Essex, and Baz McKee of the School of Oriental and African Studies. My thanks also go to students and readers who have made sporadic useful suggestions, many of which have been incorporated into this new edition.

However, this book does not necessarily represent the views of the people mentioned above, as I have not always followed their advice. I am solely responsible for any errors or over-simplifications which may remain.

One further point: in this edition, I have tried to avoid the sexist linguistic usages found in the earlier versions, which misleadingly implied in places that only males of our species could talk. I have done this partly by using the plural (*people* instead of *he*), partly by using indefinites (*a person*, *anyone*) followed by a plural pronoun (*if anyone is surprised, they should see how increasingly common this usage is*), and partly by interchanging *he* and *she* in places where a neutral between sexes pronoun is required.

JEAN AITCHISON
London School of Economics, January 1987

Acknowledgments

For permission to include copyright material in this book the author and publishers are grateful to the Estate of the late Sir Alan Herbert for a passage from *What a Word* by A. P. Herbert; and to Dr J. B. Searle for his limerick 'There was a young man of Dunlaoghaire'.

PART ONE

Starting Out

'Worry about words, Bobby. Your grandmother is right. For, whatever else you may do, you will be using words always. All day, and every day, words matter. Though you live in a barrel and speak to nobody but yourself, words matter. For words are the tools of thought . . .'

A. P. HERBERT

1

What is Linguistics?

Most people spend an immense amount of their life talking, listening, and, in advanced societies, reading and writing. Normal conversation uses 4,000 or 5,000 words an hour. A radio talk, where there are fewer pauses, uses as many as 8,000 or 9,000 words per hour. A person reading at a normal speed covers 14,000 or 15,000 words per hour. So someone who chats for an hour, listens to a radio talk for an hour and reads for an hour possibly comes into contact with 25,000 words in that time. Per day, the total could be as high as 100,000.

The use of language is an integral part of being human. Children all over the world start putting words together at approximately the same age, and follow remarkably similar paths in their speech development. All languages are surprisingly similar in their basic structure, whether they are found in South America, Australia or near the North Pole. Language and abstract thought are closely connected, and many people think that these two characteristics above all distinguish human beings from animals.

An inability to use language adequately can affect someone's status in society, and may even alter their personality. Because of its crucial importance in human life, every year an increasing number of psychologists, sociologists, anthropologists, teachers, speech therapists, computer scientists and copywriters (to name but a few professional groups) realize that they need to study language more deeply. So it is not surprising that in recent years one of the fastest-expanding branches of knowledge has been linguistics—the systematic study of language.

Linguistics tries to answer the basic questions 'What is language?' and 'How does language work?' It probes into various aspects of these problems, such as 'What do all languages have in common?',

'What range of variation is found among languages?', 'How does human language differ from animal communication?', 'How does a child learn to speak?', 'How does one write down and analyse an unwritten language?', 'Why do languages change?', 'To what extent are social class differences reflected in language?' and so on.

What is a linguist?

A person who studies linguistics is usually referred to as a **linguist**. The more accurate term 'linguistician' is too much of a tongue-twister to become generally accepted. The word 'linguist' is unsatisfactory: it causes confusion, since it also refers to someone who speaks a large number of languages. Linguists in the sense of linguistics experts need not be fluent in languages, though they must have a wide experience of different types of languages. It is more important for them to analyse and attempt to explain linguistic phenomena such as the Turkish vowel system, or German verbs, than to make themselves understood in Istanbul or Berlin. They are skilled, objective observers rather than participants—consumers of languages rather than producers, as one social scientist flippantly commented.

Our type of linguist is perhaps best likened to a musicologist. A musicologist could analyse a piano concerto by pointing out the theme and variations, harmony and counterpoint. But such a person need not actually play the concerto, a task left to the concert pianist. Music theory bears the same relation to actual music as linguistics does to language.

How does linguistics differ from traditional grammar?

One frequently meets people who think that linguistics is old school grammar jazzed up with a few new names. But it differs in several basic ways.

First, and most important, linguistics is **descriptive**, not prescriptive. Linguists are interested in what *is* said, not what they think *ought* to be said. They describe language in all its aspects, but do not prescribe rules of 'correctness'.

It is a common fallacy that there is some absolute standard of correctness which it is the duty of linguists, schoolmasters, grammars and dictionaries to maintain. There was an uproar in America when in 1961 *Webster's Third New International Dictionary of the English Language* included words such as *ain't* and phrases such as *ants in one's pants.* The editors were deliberately corrupting the language—or else they were incompetent, argued the critics. 'Webster III has thrust upon us a dismaying assortment of the questionable, the perverse, the unworthy and the downright out-rageous', said one angry reviewer. But if people say *ain't* and *ants in one's pants*, linguists consider it important to record the fact. They are observers and recorders, not judges.

'I am irritated by the frequent use of the words *different to* on radio and other programmes' ran a letter to a daily paper. 'In my schooldays of fifty years ago we were taught that things were *alike to* and *different from*. Were our teachers so terribly ignorant?' This correspondent has not realized that languages are constantly chang-ing. And the fact that he comments on the *frequent* use of *different to* indicates that it has as much right to be classified as 'correct' as *different from*.

The notion of absolute and unchanging 'correctness' is quite foreign to linguists. They might recognize that one type of speech appears, through the whim of fashion, to be more socially accept-able than others. But this does not make the socially acceptable variety any more interesting for them than the other varieties, or the old words any better than new ones. To linguists the language of a pop singer is not intrinsically worse (or better) than that of a duke. They would disagree strongly with the *Daily Telegraph* writer who complained that 'a disc jockey talking to the latest Neanderthal pop idol is a truly shocking experience of verbal squalor'. Nor do linguists condemn the coining of new words. This is a natural and continuous process, not a sign of decadence and decay. A linguist would note with interest, rather than horror, the fact that you can have your hair washed and set in a *glamorama* in North Carolina, or your car oiled at a *lubritorium* in Sydney, or that you can buy apples at a *fruitique* in a trendy suburb of London.

A second important way in which linguistics differs from tra-ditional school grammar is that linguists regard the **spoken** language as primary, not the written. In the past, grammarians have over-stressed the importance of the written word, partly because of its permanence. It was difficult to cope with fleeting utterances before the invention of sound recording. The traditional classical edu-cation was also partly to blame. People insisted on moulding language in accordance with the usage of the 'best authors' of classical times, and these authors existed only in written form. This attitude began as far back as the 2nd century B.C. when scholars in Alexandria took the authors of 5th-century Greece as their models.

This belief in the superiority of the written word has continued for over two millennia.

But linguists look first at the spoken word, which preceded the written everywhere in the world, as far as we know. Moreover, most writing systems are derived from the vocal sounds. Although spoken utterances and written sentences share many common features, they also exhibit considerable differences. Linguists therefore regard spoken and written forms as belonging to different, though overlapping systems, which must be analysed separately: the spoken first, then the written.

A third way in which linguistics differs from traditional grammar studies is that it does not force languages into a Latin-based framework. In the past, many traditional textbooks have assumed unquestioningly that Latin provides a universal framework into which all languages fit, and countless schoolchildren have been confused by meaningless attempts to force English into foreign patterns. It is sometimes claimed, for example, that a phrase such as *for John* is in the 'dative case'. But this is blatantly untrue, since English does not have a Latin-type case system. At other times, the influence of the Latin framework is more subtle, and so more misleading. Many people have wrongly come to regard certain Latin categories as being 'natural' ones. For example, it is commonly assumed that the Latin tense divisions of past, present and future are inevitable. Yet one frequently meets languages which do not make this neat threefold distinction. In some languages, it is more important to express the duration of an action—whether it is a single act or a continuing process—than to locate the action in time.

In addition, judgements on certain constructions often turn out to have a Latin origin. For example, people frequently argue that 'good English' avoids 'split infinitives' as in the phrase *to humbly apologize*, where the infinitive *to apologize* is 'split' by *humbly*. A letter to the London *Evening Standard* is typical of many: 'Do split infinitives madden your readers as much as they do me?' asks the correspondent. 'Can I perhaps ask that, at least, judges and editors make an effort to maintain the form of our language?' The idea that a split infinitive is wrong is based on Latin. Purists insist that, because a Latin infinitive is only one word, its English equivalent must be as near to one word as possible. To linguists, it is unthinkable to judge one language by the standards of another. Since split infinitives occur frequently in English, they are as 'correct' as unsplit ones.

In brief, linguists are opposed to the notion that any one language can provide an adequate framework for all the others. They are trying to set up a universal framework. And there is no reason why this should resemble the grammar of Latin, or the grammar of any other language arbitrarily selected from the thousands spoken by humans.

The scope of linguistics

Linguistics covers a wide range of topics and its boundaries are difficult to define.

A diagram in the shape of a wheel gives a rough impression of the range covered (Figure 1).

In the centre is **phonetics**, the study of human speech sounds. A good knowledge of phonetics is useful for a linguist. Yet it is a basic background knowledge, rather than part of linguistics itself.

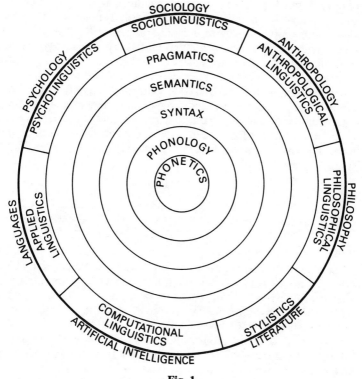

Fig. 1

Phoneticians are concerned with the actual physical sounds, the raw material out of which language is made. They study the position of the tongue, teeth and vocal cords during the production of sounds, and record and analyse sound waves. Linguists, on the other hand, are more interested in the way in which language is patterned. They analyse the shape or **form** of these patterns rather than the physical substance out of which the units of language are made. The famous Swiss linguist, Ferdinand de Saussure, expressed the difference well when he compared language with a game of chess. The linguist is interested in the various moves which the chessmen make and how they are aligned on the board. It does not matter whether the chessmen are made of wood or ivory. Their substance does not alter the rules of the game.

Although phonetics and linguistics are sometimes referred to together as 'the linguistic sciences', phonetics is not as central to general linguistics as the study of language patterning. For this reason, phonetics is omitted from this book, though some reading suggestions on phonetics are included on page 194.

In Figure 1, phonetics is surrounded by **phonology** (sound patterning), then phonology is surrounded by **syntax**. The term 'syntax', used in its broadest sense, refers to both the arrangement and the form of words. It is that part of language which links together the sound patterns and the meaning. **Semantics** (meaning) is placed outside syntax. Phonology, syntax and semantics are the 'bread and butter' of linguistics, and are a central concern of this book. Together they constitute the **grammar** of a language (Figure 2).

GRAMMAR

Fig. 2

But a word of warning about differences in terminology must be added. In some (usually older) textbooks, the word 'grammar' has a more restricted use. It refers only to what we have called the syntax. In these books, the term 'syntax' is restricted to the arrangement of words, and the standard term **morphology** is used for their make-up. This is not a case of one group of linguists being right in their use of terminology, and the other wrong, but of words gradually shifting their meaning, with the terms 'syntax' and 'grammar' extending their range.

Around the central grammatical hub comes **pragmatics**, which deals with how speakers use language in ways which cannot be predicted from linguistic knowledge alone. This relatively new and fast expanding topic has connections both with semantics, and with the various branches of linguistics which link language with the external world: **psycholinguistics** (the study of language and mind), **sociolinguistics** (the study of language and society), **applied linguistics** (the application of linguistics to language teaching), **computational linguistics** (the use of computers to simulate language and its workings), **stylistics** (the study of language and literature), **anthropological linguistics** (the study of language in cross-cultural settings), **philosophical linguistics** (the link between language and logical thought).

These various branches overlap to some extent, so are hard to define clearly. Psycholinguistics and sociolinguistics are perhaps the ones which have expanded fastest in recent years. For this reason, they are given chapters to themselves in this book.

Finally, there are two important aspects of linguistics which have been omitted from the diagram; the first is **historical linguistics**, the study of language change. This omission was inevitable in a two-dimensional diagram. But if the wheel diagram is regarded as three-dimensional, as if it were the cross-section of a tree, then we can include this topic. We can either look at a grammar at one particular point in time (a single cut across the tree), or we can study its development over a number of years, by comparing a number of different cuts made across the tree trunk at different places (Figure 3).

Because it is normally necessary to know how a system works at any one time before one can hope to understand changes, the

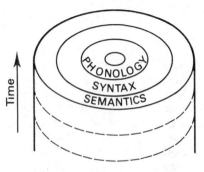

Fig. 3

analysis of language at a single point in time, or **synchronic** linguistics, is usually dealt with before historical or **diachronic** linguistics.

The second omission is **linguistic typology**, the study of different language types. This could not be fitted in because it spreads over several layers of the diagram, covering phonology, syntax, and semantics.

QUESTIONS

Test yourself on what you have read in Chapter 1 by answering the following questions:

1 How would you define **linguistics**?
2 Point out three ways in which linguistics differs from traditional school grammar.
3 What is the difference between a **prescriptive** and a **descriptive** approach to language?
4 Why do linguists regard speech rather than writing as primary?
5 Briefly explain the terms **phonology**, **syntax** and **semantics**.
6 Distinguish between **synchronic** and **diachronic** linguistics.

2

What is Language?

Linguistics can be defined as 'the systematic study of language'—a discipline which describes language in all its aspects and formulates theories as to how it works.

But what exactly *is* language? People often use the word in a very wide sense: 'the language of flowers', 'the language of music', 'body language' and so on. This book, in common with most linguistics books, uses the word to mean the specialized sound signalling system which seems to be genetically programmed to develop in humans. Humans can, of course, communicate in numerous other ways: they can wink, wave, smile, tap someone on the shoulder, and so on. This wider study, which overlaps with linguistics, is not the concern of this book. It is usually known as 'the psychology of communication', and reading on the topic is suggested on pp. 196–7.

It is also clear that humans can transfer language to various other media: written symbols, braille, sign language, and so on. Sign language in particular has interesting characteristics which are not all predictable from the spoken word. However, language based on sound is more widespread, and perhaps more basic, and so has been given priority in this book.

But can one define language? What are its characteristic features? One of the best ways to answer this question is to compare language with animal communication, and to see where the similarities and differences lie.

Use of sound signals

When animals communicate with one another, they may do so by a variety of means. Crabs, for example, communicate by waving their claws at one another, and bees have a complicated series of 'dances' which signify the whereabouts of a source of nectar.

But such methods are not as widespread as the use of sounds, which are employed by humans, grasshoppers, birds, dolphins, cows, monkeys, and many other species. So our use of sound is in no way unique. Sound signals have several advantages. They can be used in the dark, and at some distance, they allow a wide variety of messages to be sent, and they leave the body free for other activities.

Humans probably acquired their sound signalling system at a fairly late stage in their evolution. This seems likely because all the organs used in speech have some more basic function. The lungs are primarily used for breathing. Teeth, lips and tongue are primarily for eating. The vocal cords (thin strips of membrane deep in the throat) were used primarily for closing off the lungs in order to make the rib cage rigid for actions requiring a great effort. When people lift something heavy, they automatically hold their breath. This is caused by the closing of the vocal cords. The grunt when the heavy object is dropped is caused by the air being expelled as the vocal cords open. Millions of years ago we possibly needed a rigid rib cage for swinging in the trees—but humans still need this mechanism today for such actions as weightlifting, defecation and childbirth.

Arbitrariness

There is often a strong recognizable link between the actual signal and the message an animal wishes to convey. An animal who wishes to warn off an opponent may simulate an attacking attitude. A cat, for example, will arch its back, spit and appear ready to pounce.

In human language, the reverse is true. In the great majority of cases, there is no link whatsoever between the signal and the message. The symbols used are **arbitrary**. There is no intrinsic connection, for example, between the word *elephant* and the animal it symbolizes. Nor is the phrase 'These bananas are bad' intrinsically connected with food. Onomatopoeic words such as *quack-quack* and *bang* are exceptions—but there are relatively few of these compared with the total number of words.

The need for learning

Most animals automatically know how to communicate without learning. Their systems of communication are genetically inbuilt.

Bee-dancing, for example, is substantially the same in bee colonies in different parts of the world, with only small variations. Even in cases where an element of learning is involved, this is usually minor. In one experiment a chaffinch reared in a soundproof room away from other chaffinches developed an abnormal type of song. Yet when the bird was exposed to only occasional tape recordings of other chaffinches, its song developed normally.

This is quite different from the long learning process needed to acquire human language, which is culturally transmitted. A human being brought up in isolation simply does not acquire language, as is shown by the rare studies of children brought up by animals without human contact. Human language is by no means totally conditioned by the environment, and there is almost certainly some type of innate predisposition towards language in a new-born child. But this latent potentiality can only be activated by long exposure to language, which requires careful learning.

Duality

Animals who use vocal signals have a stock of basic sounds which vary according to species. A cow has under ten, a chicken has around twenty, and a fox over thirty. Dolphins have between twenty and thirty, and so do gorillas and chimpanzees. Most animals can use each basic sound only once. That is, the number of messages an animal can send is restricted to the number of basic sounds, or occasionally the basic sounds plus a few simple combinations.

Human language works rather differently. Each language has a stock of sound units or **phonemes** which are similar in number to the basic sounds possessed by animals; the average number is between thirty and forty. But each phoneme is normally meaningless in isolation. It becomes meaningful only when it is combined with other phonemes. That is, sounds such as *f*, *g*, *d*, *o*, mean nothing separately. They normally take on meaning only when they are combined together in various ways, as in *fog*, *dog*, *god*.

This organization of language into two layers—a layer of sounds which combine into a second layer of larger units—is known as **duality** or **double articulation**. A communication system with duality is considerably more flexible than one without it, because a far greater number of messages can be sent.

At one time, it was thought that duality was a characteristic unique to human language. But now some people claim that it exists also in bird song, where each individual note is meaningless. It is the combination of notes into longer sequences which constitutes a meaningful melody.

Displacement

Most animals can communicate about things in the immediate environment only. A bird utters its danger cry only when danger is present. It cannot give information about a peril which is removed in time and place. This type of spontaneous utterance is nearer to a human baby's emotional cries of pain, hunger or contentment than it is to fully developed language.

Human language, by contrast, can communicate about things that are absent as easily as about things that are present. This apparently rare phenomenon, known as **displacement**, does occasionally occur in the animal world, for example, in the communication of honey bees. If a worker bee finds a new source of nectar, it returns to the hive and performs a complex dance in order to inform the other bees of the exact location of the nectar, which may be several miles away. But even bees are limited in this ability. They can inform each other only about nectar. Human language can cope with any subject whatever, and it does not matter how far away the topic of conversation is in time and space.

Creativity (Productivity)

Most animals have a very limited number of messages they can send or receive. The male of a certain species of grasshopper, for example, has a choice of six, which might be translated as follows:

1   I am happy, life is good.
2   I would like to make love.
3   You are trespassing on my territory.
4   She's mine.
5   Let's make love.
6   Oh how nice to have made love.

Not only is the number of messages fixed for the grasshopper, but so are the circumstances under which each can be communicated. All animals, as far as we know, are limited in a similar way. Bees can communicate only about nectar. Dolphins, in spite of their intelligence and large number of clicks, whistles and squawks, seem to be restricted to communicating about the same things again and again. And even the clever vervet monkey, who is claimed to make thirty-six different vocal sounds, is obliged to repeat these over and over.

This type of restriction is not found in human language, which is essentially **creative** (or **productive**). Humans can produce novel utterances whenever they want to. A person can utter a sentence which has never been said before, in the most unlikely circumstances, and still be understood. If, at a party, someone said, 'There is a purple platypus crawling across the ceiling', friends might think the speaker was drunk, drugged, or having a nervous breakdown, but they would still understand the words spoken. Conversely, in an everyday routine situation, a person is not obliged to say the same thing every time. At breakfast, someone might say 'This is good coffee' on one day, 'Is this coffee or dandelion tea?' on the next, and 'It would be cheaper to drink petrol' on the next.

Patterning

Many animal communication systems consist of a simple list of elements. There is no internal organization within the system.

Human language, on the other hand, is most definitely not a haphazard heap of individual items. Humans do not juxtapose sounds and words in a random way. Instead, they ring the changes on a few well-defined patterns.

Take the sounds *a*, *b*, *s*, *t*. In English, there are only four possible ways in which these sounds could be arranged, *bats*, *tabs*, *stab* or *bast* 'inner bark of lime'. All other possibilities, such as **sbat*, **abts*, **stba*, are excluded (an asterisk indicates an impossible word or sentence). The starred words are not excluded in this case because such sequences are unpronounceable, but because the 'rules' subconsciously followed by people who know English do not allow these combinations, even for new words. A new washing powder called *Sbat* would be unlikely to catch on, since English does not permit the initial squence *sb*, even though in some other languages (for example, ancient Greek) this combination is not unusual.

Similarly, consider the words, *burglar*, *loudly*, *sneezed*, *the*. Here again, only three combinations are possible: *The burglar sneezed loudly*, *Loudly sneezed the burglar* and (perhaps) *The burglar loudly sneezed*. All others are impossible, such as **The loudly burglar sneezed*, or **Sneezed burglar loudly the*. Note also that had the four words been *burglars*, *a*, *sneezes*, *loudly*, there is no way in which these could be combined to make a well-formed sentence. **A* *burglars* is an impossible combination, and so is *★burglars sneezes*. In brief, English places firm restrictions on which items can occur together, and the order in which they come.

From this, it follows that there is also a fixed set of possibilities for the substitution of items. In the word *bats*, for example, *a* could be replaced by *e* or *i*, but not by *h* or *z*, which would give *★bhts* or *★bzts*. In the sentence *The burglar sneezed loudly*, the word *burglar* could be replaced by *cat*, *butcher*, *robber*, or even (in a children's story) by *engine* or *shoe*—but it could not be replaced by *into*, or *amazingly*, or *they*, which would give ill-formed sequences such as *★The into sneezed loudly* or *★The amazingly sneezed loudly*.

Every item in language, then, has its own characteristic place in the total pattern. It can combine with certain specified items, and be replaced by others (Figure 4).

```
The   – burglar  – sneezed – loudly
 |        |           |         |
 A    – robber   – coughed  – softly
 |        |           |         |
That  –   cat    –  hissed  – noisily
```

Fig. 4

Language can therefore be regarded as an intricate network of interlinked elements in which every item is held in its place and given its identity by all the other items. No item (apart from the names of some objects) has an independent validity or existence outside that pattern. The elements of language can be likened to the players in a game of soccer. A striker, or a goal-keeper, has no use or value outside the game. But placed among the other players, a striker acquires an identity and value. In the same way, linguistic items such as *the*, *been*, *very*, only acquire significance as part of a total language network.

Structure dependence

Let us now look again at the network of interlocking items which constitutes language. A closer inspection reveals another, more basic way in which language differs from animal communication.

Look at the sentences: *The penguin squawked*, *It squawked*, *The penguin which slipped on the ice squawked*. Each of these sentences has a similar basic structure consisting of a subject and a verb (Figure 5). The number of words in each sentence is no guide whatsoever to its basic structure. Simple counting operations are

The penguin	
It	squawked
The penguin which slipped on the ice	

Fig. 5

quite irrelevant to language. For example, suppose someone was trying to work out how to express the past in English. They would have no success at all if they tried out a strategy such as 'Add *-ed* to the end of the third word'. They might, accidentally, produce a few good sentences such as:

Uncle Herbert toasted seventeen crumpets.

But more often, the results would be quite absurd:

*Clarissa hate frogs-ed.
*The girl who-ed hate frogs scream.

In fact, it is quite impossible for anybody to form sentences and understand them unless they realize that each one has an inaudible, invisible structure, which cannot be discovered by mechanical means such as counting. Once a person has realized this, they can locate the component to which the past tense *-ed* must be added even if they have never heard or said the sentence before, and even if it contains a totally new verb, as in:

The penguin shramped the albatross.

In other words, language operations are **structure dependent**—they depend on an understanding of the internal structure of a sentence, rather than on the number of elements involved. This may seem obvious to speakers of English. But the rarity, or perhaps absence, of this property in animal communication indicates its crucial importance. Its presence has not been proved in any animal system (though bird song may turn out to be structure dependent, according to some researchers).

Moreover, the types of structure dependent operations found in language are often quite complicated, and involve considerably more than the mere addition of items (as in the case of the past tense). Elements of structure can change places, or even be omitted. For example, in one type of question, the first verbal element changes places with the subject:

[*That dirty child*] [*must*] *wash,*

has the related question

[*Must*] [*that dirty child*] *wash?*

And in the sentence,

Billy swims faster than Henrietta.

it is generally agreed that the sentence means 'Billy swims faster than Henrietta swims', and that the second occurrence of *swims* is 'understood'.

Such sophistication is mind-boggling compared with the thirty-six cries of the vervet monkey, or even the relatively complex dances by which bees indicate the whereabouts of honey to their colleagues.

Human language versus animal communication

So far, the main similarities and differences between human and animal communication can be summed up as follows:

Human language is a signalling system which uses sounds, a characteristic shared by a large number of animal systems. In animal communication, there is frequently a connection between the signal and the message sent, and the system is mainly genetically inbuilt. In human language, the symbols are mostly arbitrary, and the system has to be painstakingly transmitted from one generation to another. Duality and displacement—the organization of language into two layers, and the ability to talk about absent objects and events—are extremely rare in the animal world. No animal communication system has both these features. Creativity, the ability to produce novel utterances, seems not to be present in any natural communication system possessed by animals. Finally, patterning and structure dependence may also be unique language features.

To summarize: language is a patterned system of arbitrary sound signals, characterized by structure dependence, creativity, displacement, duality, and cultural transmission.

This is true of all languages in the world, which are remarkably similar in their main design features. There is no evidence that any language is more 'primitive' than any other. There are certainly primitive cultures. A primitive culture is reflected in the vocabulary of a language, which might lack words common in advanced societies. But even the most primitive tribes have languages whose underlying structure is every bit as complex as English or Russian or Chinese.

Origin and functions of language

Language, as we have seen, seems to be a highly developed form of animal signalling. But there is a missing link in the chain. How, and when, did we start to talk?

This is a problem of interest mainly to ethologists (students of animal behaviour), and one which has not yet been solved. Most linguists regard this fascinating topic as being outside the realm of linguistics proper. They are more interested in studying actual language than in speculating about its remote origins.

But although *how* language began is a puzzle, *why* language began seems rather clearer. Possibly it began because humans needed a greater degree of cooperation with each other in order to survive, and this cooperation required efficient communication. Consequently, the primary function of language is to impart factual information and to convey essential commands.

But language can also be used to communicate feelings and emotions. This aspect of language is not as well developed as 'information talking', because humans, like other primates, can convey emotions by screams, grunts, sobs, gestures and so on. So they need language only to confirm and elaborate these more primitive signals. In addition, there is the language of social chit-chat, the meaningless small talk of everyday life. 'Hallo, how nice to see you. How are you? Isn't the weather terrible?' This social patter has been called **phatic communion** and is primarily a device to maintain social contact on a friendly level. Some ethologists call it 'grooming talking' and suggest that it is a substitute for the friendly grooming indulged in by monkeys.

There are other biologically less important functions of language. Humans may use language for purely aesthetic reasons. In writing poetry, for example, people manipulate words in the same way as they might model clay or paint a picture. Or they may talk in order to release nervous tension, a function seen when people mutter to themselves in anger and frustration.

QUESTIONS

1 Suggest at least three properties of language which are rare or absent in animal communication.
2 What is meant by **creativity**?

3 What is meant by **structure dependence**?
4 Work out how many ways the words *surprisingly*, *eggs*, *eat*, *elephants*, *large*, *will*, *sometimes* can be arranged to produce well-formed English sentences.
5 Suggest some reasons why people talk.

3

The Study of Language

The discipline of linguistics can be likened to a pathway which is being cut through the dark and mysterious forest of language. Different parts of the forest have been explored at different times, so we can depict the path as a winding one.

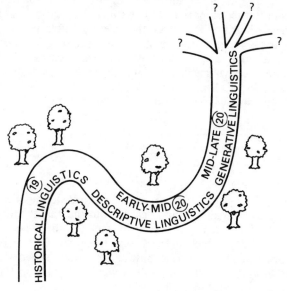

Fig. 6

As Figure 6 shows, there have been three major directions in linguistics in the past two centuries. Let us discuss each of these in more detail.

Nineteenth century: historical linguistics

Before the 19th century, language in the western world was of interest mainly to philosophers. It is significant that the Greek philosophers Plato and Aristotle made major contributions to the study of language. Plato, for example, is said to have been the first person to distinguish between nouns and verbs.

1786 is the year which many people regard as the birthdate of linguistics. On the 27th of September, 1786, an Englishman, Sir William Jones, read a paper to the Royal Asiatic Society in Calcutta pointing out that Sanskrit (the old Indian language), Greek, Latin, Celtic and Germanic all had striking structural similarities. So impressive were these likenesses that these languages must spring from one common source, he concluded. Although Jones has the credit of making this discovery, it was an idea that was occurring independently to several scholars at the same time.

Sir William Jones' discovery fired the imagination of scholars. For the next hundred years, all other linguistic work was eclipsed by the general preoccupation with writing comparative grammars, grammars which first compared the different linguistic forms found in the various members of the Indo-European language family, and second, attempted to set up a hypothetical ancestor, Proto-Indo-European, from which all these languages were descended. (Figure 7 below excludes Hittite and Tocharian, which were not recognized as Indo-European languages until the 20th century.)

Fig. 7

The 19th-century concern with reconstructing Proto-Indo-European, and making hypotheses about the way it split into the various modern languages, was encouraged by the general intellectual climate of the times. In the mid-19th century, Darwin published his famous *Origin of Species*, putting forward the theory of evolution. It seemed natural to attempt to chart the evolution of language alongside the evolution of species.

This emphasis on language change eventually led to a major theoretical advance. In the last quarter of the century, a group of scholars centred around Leipzig, and nicknamed the 'Young Grammarians', claimed that language change is 'regular'. They argued that if, in any word of a given dialect, one sound changes into another, the change will also affect all other occurrences of the same sound in similar phonetic surroundings. For example, in Old English the word *chin* was pronounced 'kin' (spelt *cinn*). This change from a *k*-sound to *ch* affected all other *k*-sounds which occurred at the beginning of a word before *e* or *i*. So we also get *chicken*, *child*, *chide*, *chip*, *chill*, *cheese*, *cheek*, *chest*, *chew* and so on—all of which originally had a *k*-sound at the beginning. Although, today, the claims made by the Young Grammarians have been modified to some extent (as will be discussed in Chapter 12), it was an important step forward for linguists to realize that language changes were not just optional tendencies, but definite and clearly stateable 'laws' (as the Young Grammarians perhaps misleadingly called them).

The influence of the 19th-century scholars was strong. Even today, one still meets members of the general public who expect the cataloguing of linguistic changes and the reconstruction of Proto-Indo-European to be the central concern of modern linguistics.

Early- to mid-20th century: descriptive linguistics

In the 20th century, the emphasis shifted from language change to language description. Instead of looking at how a selection of items changed in a number of different languages, linguists began to concentrate on describing single languages at one particular point in time.

If any one person can be held responsible for this change of emphasis, it was the Swiss scholar Ferdinand de Saussure (1857–1913), who is sometimes labelled 'the father of modern linguistics'. Amazingly, he died without having written any major work on general linguistics. But his students collected together his lecture notes after his death and published them under the title *Course in General Linguistics* (1915), which exerted a major influence on the course of linguistics, particularly in Europe.

De Saussure's crucial contribution was his explicit and reiterated statement that all language items are essentially interlinked. This was an aspect of language which had not been stressed before. Nobody had seriously examined the relationship of each element to all the others. As noted earlier, it was de Saussure who first suggested that language was like a game of chess, a system in which each item is defined by its relationship to all the others. His insistence that language is a carefully built **structure** of interwoven elements initiated the era of **structural linguistics**.

The term 'structural linguistics' is sometimes misunderstood. It does not necessarily refer to a separate branch or school of linguistics. *All* linguistics since de Saussure is structural, as 'structural' in this broad sense merely means the recognition that language is a patterned system composed of interdependent elements, rather than a collection of unconnected individual items. Misunderstandings sometimes arise because the label 'structuralist' is often attached to the descriptive linguists who worked in the USA between 1930 and 1960. Let us now turn to these.

In America, linguistics began as an offshoot of anthropology. Around the beginning of the 20th century, anthropologists were eager to record the culture of the fast-dying American-Indian tribes, and the American-Indian languages were one aspect of this. Although often interesting, the work of those early scholars was, for the most part, haphazard and lacking cohesion. There were no firm guidelines for linguists to follow when they attempted to describe exotic languages. This state of affairs changed with the publication in 1933 of Leonard Bloomfield's comprehensive work entitled simply *Language*, which attempted to lay down rigorous procedures for the description of any language.

Bloomfield considered that linguistics should deal objectively and systematically with observable data. So he was more interested in the way items were arranged than in meaning. The study of meaning was not amenable to rigorous methods of analysis and was therefore, he concluded, 'the weak point in language study, and will remain so until human knowledge advances very far beyond its present state'.

Bloomfield had immense influence—far more than the European linguists working during this period—and the so-called 'Bloomfieldian era' lasted for more than twenty years. During this time, large numbers of linguists concentrated on writing descriptive grammars of unwritten languages. This involved first finding native speakers of the language concerned and collecting sets of utterances from them. Second, it involved analysing the corpus of collected utterances by studying the phonological and syntactic patterns of the language concerned, as far as possible without recourse to meaning. Items were (in theory) identified and classified solely on the basis of their distribution within the corpus.

In the course of writing such grammars, a number of problems arose which could not be solved by the methods proposed by Bloomfield. So an enormous amount of attention was paid to the refinement of analytical techniques. For many, the ultimate goal of linguistics was the perfection of **discovery procedures**—a set of principles which would enable a linguist to 'discover' (or perhaps more accurately, 'uncover') in a foolproof way the linguistic units of an unwritten language. Because of their overriding interest in the internal patterns or 'structure' of the language, such linguists are sometimes labelled 'structuralists'.

The Bloomfieldians laid down a valuable background of linguistic methodology for future generations. But linguistics also became very narrow. Trivial problems of analysis became major controversial issues, and no one who was not a linguist could understand the issues involved. By around 1950 linguistics had lost touch with other disciplines and become an abstruse subject of little interest to anyone outside it. It was ready for a revolution.

Mid- to late-20th century: generative linguistics and the search for universals

In 1957, linguistics took a new turning. Noam Chomsky, then aged twenty-nine, a teacher at the Massachusetts Institute of Technology, published a book called *Syntactic Structures*. Although containing fewer than 120 pages, this little book started a revolution in linguistics. Chomsky is, arguably, the most influential linguist of the century. Certainly, he is the linguist whose reputation has spread furthest outside linguistics. He has, in the opinion of many, transformed linguistics from a relatively obscure discipline of interest mainly to PhD students and future missionaries into a major social science of direct relevance to psychologists, sociologists, anthropologists, philosophers and others.

Chomsky has shifted attention away from detailed descriptions of actual utterances, and started asking questions about the nature of the system which produces the output.

According to Chomsky, Bloomfieldian linguistics was both far too ambitious and far too limited in scope. It was too ambitious in that it was unrealistic to expect to be able to lay down foolproof rules for extracting a perfect description of a language from a mass of data. It was too limited because it concentrated on describing sets of utterances which happened to have been spoken.

A grammar, he claimed, should be more than a description of old utterances. It should also take into account possible future utterances. In short, the traditional viewpoint that the main task of linguists is simply to describe a corpus of actual utterances cannot account for the characteristic of productivity, or **creativity**, as

Chomsky prefers to call it. This, as we noted in Chapter 2, is the ability of human beings to produce and comprehend an indefinite number of novel utterances.

Chomsky points out that anyone who knows a language must have internalized a set of rules which specify the sequences permitted in their language. In his opinion, a linguist's task is to discover these rules, which constitute the grammar of the language in question. Chomsky therefore uses the word 'grammar' interchangeably to mean, on the one hand, a person's internalized rules, and on the other hand, a linguist's guess as to these rules. (This is perhaps confusing, as the actual rules in a person's mind are unlikely to be the same as a linguist's hypothesis, even though there will probably be some overlap).

A grammar which consists of a set of statements or **rules** which specify which sequences of a language are possible, and which impossible, is a **generative** grammar. Chomsky, therefore, initiated the era of generative linguistics. In his words, a grammar will be 'a device which generates all the grammatical sequences of a language and none of the ungrammatical ones'. Such a grammar is perfectly **explicit**, in that nothing is left to the imagination. The rules must be precisely formulated in such a way that anyone would be able to separate the well-formed sentences from the ill-formed ones, even if they did not know a word of the language concerned. The particular type of generative grammar favoured by Chomsky is a so-called **transformational** one. The basic characteristics of **transformational-generative grammar** (TGG) are outlined in Chapters 14–16.

Chomsky has not only initiated the era of generative grammars. He has also redirected attention towards **language universals**. He points out that as all humans are rather similar, their internalized language mechanisms are likely to have important common properties. He argues that linguists should concentrate on finding elements and constructions that are *available* to all languages, whether or not they actually occur. Above all, they should seek to specify the universal bounds or **constraints** within which human language operates.

The constraints on human language are, he suggests, inherited ones. Human beings may well be pre-programmed with a basic knowledge of what languages in general are like, and how they work. Chomsky has given the label **Universal Grammar** (UG) to this inherited core, and he regards it as a major task of linguistics to specify what it consists of.

Chomsky is not the only linguist to have made proposals about generative grammar and universal frameworks. The search for a universal generative grammar is a general characteristic of theoretical linguistics at the present time, and various proposals have been made. Chomsky's theories, however, are those which have received the most widespread attention in the past quarter century, even though it is possible that, after more research, one of the less well-known rival systems (briefly mentioned in Chapter 16) will turn out to be superior.

An explosion of interest in language among non-linguists has been a valuable by-product of Chomsky's work. The emphasis within linguistics has turned to the language potential of human beings in general, rather than the detailed description of single languages. As a result, huge numbers of psychologists, neurologists, anthropologists, sociologists, philosophers, to name just a few, have begun to take a greater interest in language and linguistics. Collaboration between linguists and these other social scientists has led to the development of what were once considered 'fringe areas', such as psycholinguistics and sociolinguistics, but are now major fields in their own right.

QUESTIONS

1 Why were 19th century linguists so interested in historical linguistics?
2 Why is de Saussure an important figure in linguistics?
3 What are **discovery procedures**?
4 What is a **generative** grammar, and how does it differ from a **descriptive** grammar?
5 Explain the word **explicit** when used in connection with grammars.

4

Deciding Where to Begin

Language is an enormous and very complex phenomenon. If one wants to study it, where should one begin? People tend to argue about this. Let us therefore consider the various possibilities. First, however, it may be useful to discuss why people disagree over the best way to go about it.

Language as a game

Language can be regarded as a complicated type of game, assuming a 'game' to be 'a specified type of activity governed by rules'. The various facets involved in a game can reveal some of the problems faced by linguists, and show why there is some argument when they try to decide where to begin studying language.

In a typical game, such as chess or soccer, anyone trying to find out how the game is played has to deal with three broad types of question: the *aims of the game*, the *principles of interaction*, and the *permitted moves*.

Under the **aims of the game**, comes the fundamental question: what are people trying to do when they play it? In soccer, the players are trying to kick the ball into a net in order to score. The 'aims' of language involve not only the broad functions outlined in Chapter 2 (conveying information, expressing emotion, keeping in touch socially, and so on), but also more specific purposes for which language can be used, such as:

Obtain information: *Where's the parrot?*
Make someone do something: *Shut the door!*
Make a promise: *I'll pay you next week.*

The **principles of interaction** involve questions such as: How many people can play? Do they all play at the same time, or do they take it in turns? If so, how does one know when a person's turn is over? Within language, people take it in turns to speak, and each language tends to have certain socially prescribed 'turns'. For example, in English, a greeting is usually followed by another greeting:

John: *Good morning, Felicity.*
Felicity: *Why hello there, John.*

Under **permitted moves**, one considers which 'moves' are permitted, and which not. In chess, some pieces can move across the board only in straight lines, and others only diagonally. With regard to language, there are rules underlying well-formed sequences of a language. In English, for example, verbs precede their objects, as in *The cat ate the canary*, rather than **The cat the canary ate* which would be the standard order in, say, Turkish.

All of these aspects of a game are important, and no-one could play the game without some acquaintance with them. In language also, all these facets are relevant, and native speakers have a knowledge of all of them.

When dealing with language, one might at first sight want to tackle these facets in the order listed above. But in practice, there is a problem. It is easier to specify the basic permitted moves than it is to give an equivalent account of the aims and principles of interaction, which are closely interwoven with the social structures of the society involved. For this reason, the majority of professional linguists prefer to begin with those aspects of language which can most easily be detached from the social background. They therefore start with the permitted moves or, in linguistic terminology, the grammar of the language. They consider this to be the core of linguistic study, and expect to add on its interrelationships with other facets of language and society at a later stage. Furthermore, most people find that, without a knowledge of basic linguistic principles, they can talk only in generalities about the other related facets. A knowledge of the linguistic resources of a language is often a prerequisite to an intelligent discussion of how these resources are used.

In this book, therefore, we shall be moving from the basic linguistic core outwards, in other words, we shall start from the centre of the circle diagram shown in Chapter 1, and move out to the edges later. But a decision as to where to begin does not necessarily imply an overall order of importance: people put on their socks before their shoes, but they are not necessarily attributing greater importance to socks than to shoes.

Universal and particular

Controversy does not necessarily cease even among those who agree that it is useful to begin studying language by looking at the three central components which make up a grammar: phonology, syntax and semantics (Figure 8). In general, people fall into one of two categories. On the one hand, there are those who want to study language because they are interested in knowing more about one particular language. Into this first category might come a teacher of French, or a missionary who had discovered a new South American language, or a person who has an American-Indian great-grandmother and wants to know more about Nootka. On the other hand, there are those who want to find out more about language as such. Into this second category come the majority of professional linguists and other social scientists—people such as sociologists, psychologists and anthropologists, who need to know about the phenomenon of language as a whole.

Fig. 8

These two groups of people are likely to write very different types of grammar, and to view linguistics quite differently. Those interested in a particular language will be trying to write a perfect grammar of that language (or one section of it), usually by making a detailed study of the patterns of that language alone. For example, they might be interested in the relationship of French vowels to one another. It would be quite irrelevant to them whether this vowel system coincided with that of any other language, and such people would probably pick those aspects of linguistics to help them which seemed to be best suited to the phenomenon they were examining, even if it meant choosing an unfashionable or unknown model of grammar. They are likely to consider that the chief role of linguistics is the development of analytic techniques which will enable them to fulfil their chosen task.

Those interested in language as a whole, on the other hand, will be trying to lay down a grammatical framework which will be suitable for all languages. Although such people may well write a grammar of a particular language, they will be doing this in order to test out a theory with wider implications, since one way of testing a proposed universal framework is to see whether it will fit any given language. If it does not, then it must be amended or abandoned. This type of person might also be working on French vowels, but they would be interested not so much in the vowels themselves, as in finding a framework which could 'capture' their peculiarities along-side those of other languages. A framework which was perfect for French, but was inadequate for, say, Greek, Swahili and Icelandic, would have to be abandoned.

Unfortunately, in recent years, extremists from each of these groups of people have spent an unnecessary amount of time attack-ing one another. Those interested in a particular language have argued that those searching for a universal framework are too theoretical and irrelevant to everyday life. One hears comments such as, 'Modern linguistics doesn't help me very much when it comes to teaching my Spanish class', and 'I'm doing a thesis on fish imagery in Shakespeare, and I can't see where linguistics fits in'. The 'universalists' counter this criticism by saying that the 'particu-larists' are narrow-minded people who simply like collecting facts, and one hears comments such as, 'I wish she'd stop making lists of irregular verbs in Arawak and get on with something useful'.

As will be clear from Chapter 3, the reasons for this controversy are partly historical. It is characteristic of an academic discipline to take new turnings: the 'old' school will regard the new with suspicion and distaste, and the 'new' will condemn the old as misguided and out of date. Since those who are interested in individual languages have very similar aims to the Bloomfieldian descriptivists, they tend to be treated as old-fashioned by the universalists, who are often convinced that they are 'right' merely because their type of linguistics is currently more fashionable.

In fact, the universalist and particularist views are com-plementary, not contradictory. No one can work seriously on a universal framework unless they have at their disposal a consider-able amount of information about individual languages against which to test their theories. Conversely, the heaping up of masses of information about diverse languages reduces linguistics to the level of a hobby such as stamp-collecting unless some attempt is made to relate the miscellaneous facts within a wider framework.

Moreover, it is perhaps wrong to assume that anyone interested in linguistics *must* fall into either the particularist or the universalist category. Nowadays, a growing number of people are carrying out both types of study. In addition, those who start out with an interest in a particular language ideally move on to becoming interested in language as such. The progression from a predilection for, say, German word formation or French vowels, to a desire to help develop a universal grammatical framework can be likened to the possible progression of an intelligent motor mechanic, who is likely to move from a wish to service their own car, to an interest in how cars work in general. A person may, initially, want to learn only how to fit a new fan-belt on to a Rolls-Royce. This may lead them to an interest in identifying and labelling the various components of the car's engine, and an understanding of how they fit together. Eventually, they may become curious as to how the Rolls-Royce compares with other cars, and to start looking into the theory of the internal-combustion engine as a whole.

The progression from the particular to the universal is perhaps more important for the linguist than for the motor mechanic. Anyone working seriously on a language is likely to need to know whether the phenomena they meet are unique or commonplace. To take a trivial example, someone working on English may be intrigued by the division of nouns into those that can be counted, as in *six hens*, *three cabbages*, and those that cannot: we do not normally say *six butters*, or *three soaps* (unless we mean three types of butter or soap). We have to say *some butter, some soap,* or use a word expressing a quantity, as in *six pounds of butter, three bars of soap.* How widespread is this phenomenon in the languages of the world? Is English exceptional in this respect? Or is, say, Igbo exceptional in not having such a distinction? Furthermore, if a language *does* make this distinction, are there any other related characteristics which are likely to follow in consequence? These are the types of question which, in the short run, are likely to lead someone to study language in a wider way.

In the long run, a 'universal grammar' (if one could ever be written) would have enormously important implications for our knowledge of the human race. Such a grammar might well reflect innate properties of the human mind. In the opinion of Chomsky, 'There are very deep and restrictive principles that determine the nature of human language and are rooted in the specific character of the human mind'.

However, the search for a universal grammar poses a problem for those starting out on linguistics. All proposals concerning trans-formational grammar, or any other suggested type of universal framework, are in such a state of flux that it is quite unrealistic to expect everyone to be aware of the latest proposed amendments to such a theory, which changes all the time. Because of the technical, and perhaps ephemeral nature of much recent work, this topic has been placed at the end of the book (Chapters 14–16). These chapters can be ignored by those interested only in a particular language, but are essential reading for people who want to delve further into current theories on language and linguistics.

It is, then, important for anyone studying linguistics to have a basic background knowledge of the techniques of descriptive linguistics, particularly the procedures and terminology used in the identification of basic linguistic items. The use of such techniques is essential if one is faced with a hitherto unknown, unwritten lan-guage, where the flow of speech must be broken down into seg-ments. They can be of value in other circumstances also. Language teachers, for example, may gain new insights into the languages they teach if they approach them as if they were totally new, unwritten languages. Such people need to know the answers to such questions as: 'How can one identify words?', 'What is a word?', 'Can a word be split up into smaller segments? If so, by what criteria can one do this?', 'How is it possible to identify the basic sounds in any language?', and so on. These and similar questions will be dealt with in the next few chapters.

To return to the wheel diagram discussed in Chapter 1, we will first of all deal with the inner circles of phonology, syntax and semantics (Chapters 5–8). We will then move on to the outer rings, looking in turn at pragmatics, sociolinguistics and psycholinguistics (Chapters 9–11). We shall then consider areas which did not fit into the circle diagram, language change and language comparison, including typology (Chapters 12–13). Finally, we shall turn to Chomsky's proposals for a universal framework (Chapters 14–16).

QUESTIONS

1 Why is language like a game?
2 Which aspects of a language are most easily detachable from social structures?
3 Why is someone working on a single language likely to want to widen out this study?

PART TWO

The Inner Circles

Alice was too much puzzled to say anything, so after a minute Humpty Dumpty began again. 'They've a temper, some of them—particularly verbs, they're the proudest—adjectives you can do anything with, but not verbs—however, I can manage the whole lot!'

LEWIS CARROLL

5

Sound Patterns

There was a young man of Dunlaoghaire,
Who propounded an interesting theoghaire,
*   That the language of Erse*
*   Has a shortage of verse*
As the spelling makes poets so weoghaire.

                              J. B. SEARLE

Linguistics is concerned primarily with the spoken word. So a priority task for anyone describing sounds is to decide how to represent the flow of speech. Clearly, the conventional written forms are most unsatisfactory, since they often provide little guide to pronunciation. The limerick quoted above suggests that Erse (Irish Gaelic) contains many spelling eccentricities, and some of the idiosyncrasies of English written forms are illustrated by Bernard Shaw's somewhat exaggerated claim that *ghoti* could spell 'fish', with *gh* as in 'rough', *o* as in 'women', and *ti* as in 'station'! As de Saussure pointed out, 'Written forms obscure our view of language. They are not so much a garment as a disguise'.

Linguists, then, when they are concerned with sounds, abandon conventional spelling for the purpose of representing spoken utterances, and use one of the many specially devised systems of notation in which one symbol represents one sound. Perhaps the best known of these is the International Phonetic Alphabet (IPA). A number of IPA symbols are borrowed from the conventional written alphabet:

    [b] as in '*b*ird'
    [d] as in '*d*og'

(Note that the symbols representing sounds are put into square brackets.)

Other symbols are variations of alphabet letters:

[ɒ] as in 'h*o*t' is an upside down *a*.
[ŋ] as in 'ba*ng*' is a combination of *n* and *g*.
[ɪ] as in 'h*i*t' is a small-size capital ɪ.

Sometimes obsolete letters are used:

[ʃ] as in di*sh*.

Other symbols are from the Greek alphabet:

[θ] as in *th*in,

and a few symbols are inventions:

[ɬ] Welsh *ll* as in *Ll*anel*l*y.

Sometimes supplementary marks (known as 'diacritics') are added to the symbols. For example, two dots indicate length:

[u:] (long *u*) as in b*oo*t.

By such means, the IPA has built up a store of symbols which can, in theory, represent any sound in any language.

This book uses IPA symbols whenever a phonetic transcription is essential. However, as explained in Chapter 1, a knowledge of phonetics is considered to be a prerequisite for linguistics, rather than an essential part of linguistics itself. So this chapter does not contain any further information on the topic. For those who are interested, a number of elementary textbooks on the subject are recommended on page 194. Furthermore, since phonetic symbols make a text more difficult to read, this book (in common with most other linguistic textbooks) uses the conventional written letters wherever possible, even though it is the spoken form which is being discussed.

Sorting out the basic sounds

Let us assume that a linguist is working on a hitherto unknown, unwritten language. The first step is to find a suitable informant—a reliable native speaker from whom to gather samples of speech. The early sessions will concentrate on the accurate transcription of sounds, dealing at first with single words. The linguist will do this by asking the informant to name everyday objects such as *nose*, *mouth*, *house*, *tree*, *sun*, and will then transcribe each of these words in as much detail as possible. At first even sneezes and hiccups should be recorded in case they are relevant. In Zulu, for example, there are sounds known as 'clicks' which an English speaker might well overlook, since they are totally unlike any English speech sounds. The nearest equivalents are the clicking *gee-up* sounds which people make to horses, and the *tut-tut* click of disapproval.

As time goes by, and as the sounds of the language under investigation become familiar, the linguist will transcribe more and more accurately. Simultaneously, it will slowly become apparent that the variety of strange sounds is not infinite. Instead, the informant is ringing the changes on a relatively small number of basic sounds or **phonemes**, each of which may have several variant forms.

The number of phonemes varies from language to language. The average is around thirty-five. English has forty-four, according to Gimson's well-known analysis of one widely spoken variety of British English (see Further Reading, p. 194), though different accents, and different methods of analysis can result in a slightly lower number. Hawaiian, it has been claimed, has only thirteen, and one of the languages of the northern Caucasus is reported to have eighty-nine. But these extremes are unusual, and the information may be unreliable.

A **phoneme** is the smallest segment of sound which can distinguish two words. Take the words *pit* and *bit*. These differ only in their initial sound, *pit* begins with /p/ and *bit* begins with /b/. This is the smallest amount by which these two words could differ and still remain distinct forms. Any smaller subdivision would be impossible, because English does not subdivide /p/ or /b/. Similarly, take the words *pet* and *pit*. These differ only in the vowel. Once again, this is the smallest amount by which these two words could differ. There is no English sound halfway between /e/ and /ɪ/. Therefore /p/, /b/, /e/, /ɪ/ are all phonemes of English. (Note that the symbols for phonemes are normally put into slanted brackets.) Pairs of words such as *pit* and *bit*, *pit* and *pet* which differ by only one phoneme are known as **minimal pairs**, and one way to identify the phonemes of any language is to look for minimal pairs.

The phonemes of English

Let us now list the phonemes of one widely spoken variety of British English. This is the accent sometimes known as 'Received Pronunciation' (RP). It is only one of the many accents found in Great Britain, but is perhaps the most widespread. As noted above, there are forty-four phonemes, according to one common analysis. They can be divided into two types: consonants and vowels. The latter can be subdivided into relatively **pure** or unchanging vowels, as in b*i*t, b*e*t, b*a*t, b*u*t, and **diphthongs** or gliding vowels, in which the voice glides from one vowel to another, as in b*oa*t, b*uy*, b*ay*.

Consonants	*Vowels*
/p/ as in *p*ill	/æ/ as in p*a*t
/b/ as in *b*ill	/ɑː/ as in p*ar*t
/t/ as in *t*in	/e/ as in p*e*t
/d/ as in *d*in	/ɪ/ as in p*i*t
/k/ as in *c*ot	/iː/ as in p*ea*t
/g/ as in *g*ot	/ɒ/ as in p*o*t
/m/ as in *m*eat	/ɔː/ as in p*or*t
/n/ as in *n*eat	/ʊ/ as in p*u*t
/ŋ/ as in si*ng*	/uː/ as in b*oo*t
/l/ as in *l*ake	/ʌ/ as in b*u*t
/r/ as in *r*ake	/ɜː/ as in b*ir*d
/f/ as in *f*ast	/ə/ as in *a*go
/v/ as in *v*ast	/eɪ/ as in b*ay*
/θ/ as in *th*in	/aɪ/ as in b*uy*
/ð/ as in *th*en	/ɔɪ/ as in b*oy*
/s/ as in *s*ink	/aʊ/ as in b*out*
/z/ as in *z*inc	/əʊ/ as in b*oat*
/ʃ/ as in *sh*ip	/ɪə/ as in be*er*
/ʒ/ as in bei*g*e	/ɛə/ as in b*are*
/h/ as in *h*at	/ʊə/ as in d*oer*, d*our*.
/tʃ/ as in *ch*in	
/dʒ/ as in *g*in	
/w/ as in *w*et	
/j/ as in *y*et	

Allophones

Anyone working on an unwritten language must not only make a list of the phonemes of that language. They must also discover their variant forms or **allophones**. In fact, an essential part of the phoneme identification process consists of finding out which variant sounds 'belong' to each phoneme.

The amount of variation differs from phoneme to phoneme. For example, the very slight alterations in the pronunciation of English /s/ are mostly imperceptible and unimportant, whereas the variants of English /l/ are noticeable even to the untrained ear.

Sometimes the variation is random: no two sounds can ever be exactly the same, no matter how hard a speaker tries to replicate one. These slight differences normally pass unnoticed. When sounds vary randomly in this way, they are said to be in **free variation**.

At other times, the variation is predictable. The way a phoneme is pronounced can be conditioned by the sounds round it, or by its position in the word. Take the English phoneme /p/. When it occurs at the beginning of a word, it is pronounced with aspiration (a puff of breath). After /s/, this puff of breath disappears. This can be tested by holding a sheet of paper in front of the mouth and saying the words *spot*, *spill*, *pot*, *pill*. In the case of *spot* and *spill*, the paper remains motionless. But when *pot* and *pill* are pronounced, the accompanying puff of breath makes the paper billow out. In short, the aspirated variant [pʰ] and the unaspirated one [p] are both allophones of the phoneme /p/, and each occurs in a different and predictable set of environments.

A neat (and currently fashionable) way to express this is to take one variant as more basic than the other(s), and to state the circumstances under which any change in the basic form occurs. If we regard [p] as basic, we can then say that [p] changes into [pʰ] at the beginning of a word. This can be stated briefly as follows:

$p \rightarrow p^h/\# \underline{\quad}$. That is:

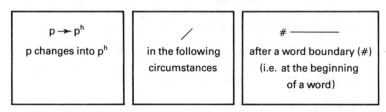

Fig. 9

Or, to take another example, consider the English phoneme /l/. This has one form at the beginning of a word, and another form at the end. In a word such as *lip*, the first consonant is a 'clear' *l*, pronounced by placing the tip of the tongue just behind the teeth and keeping the back of the tongue fairly low. In *pill*, the tongue tip is in the same place, but the back of the tongue is raised, resulting in a 'dark' *l*. So the 'clear' variant [l] and the 'dark' variant [ɫ] are both allophones of the phoneme /l/. If we regard [l] as basic, we can say that [l] changes to [ɫ] at the end of a word:

l → ł/ —— #. That is:

Fig. 10

(The distribution of these allophones is in fact more complex than the above paragraph suggests. For further information, see the books recommended on page 194.)

Sound combinations

In addition to identifying and analysing the phonemes of a language, a linguist must also work out ways in which the phonemes may be combined. Every language has certain permitted sequences of sounds, and others which are not allowed.

In English, for example, a word which begins with three consonant-type phonemes always obeys three strict rules:

1   The first phoneme must be /s/.
2   The second phoneme must be /p/ or /t/ or /k/.
3   The third phoneme must be /l/ or /r/ or /w/ or /j/.

The result is that all words beginning with three consonants are words such as *spring*, *string*, *squeal*, *splendid* or *stew*. We never find words such as **bdling*, **sgteal* or **wbtendid*.

Shared properties of phonemes

In our discussion so far, we have regarded phonemes as separate, independent units, each one having its own allophones (Figure 11):

Fig. 11

It would, however, be a mistake to regard the phonemes of English as being totally separate from one another, just as it would be a mistake to regard the members of a human family as being totally different. Even though each individual in a family is a distinct person in their own right, family members are nevertheless likely to have certain genes in common with their brothers and sisters. Similarly, many phonemes share common features.

Take the English phonemes, /p/, /t/, /b/, /d/, /m/, /n/. First, these all share the property of being **consonants**. Second, /b/, /d/, /m/, /n/ are all **voiced**—that is, they are pronounced with vibration of the vocal cords. If you put a hand on your Adam's apple and say the words *bet, debt, met, net*, you can feel this happening. You can also feel the vibration stopping when you get to the /t/ at the end. Third, /p/, /b/, /m/, are pronounced with the lips, and so share the property of being **labials** (from the Latin word for 'lip'). Fourth, when /m/ and /n/ are spoken, air is expelled through the nose. They are therefore both **nasals** (from the Latin word for 'nose'). And so on. The list of shared properties could continue for some time. However, linguists differ quite considerably as to which features they consider important. 'Labial', for example, is sometimes omitted, and a combination of other features used in its place.

We can draw up a chart which shows the properties possessed by each phoneme (Figure 12). A 'plus' sign indicates the presence of a certain property, and a 'minus' sign signifies its absence:

	/p/	/t/	/b/	/d/	/m/	/n/
Consonantal	+	+	+	+	+	+
Voiced	−	−	+	+	+	+
Labial	+	−	+	−	+	−
Nasal	−	−	−	−	+	+

Fig. 12

The more usual linguistic term for 'property' or 'component' of a phoneme is the word **feature**. So we might describe the phoneme /n/ by saying that it has the features **consonantal, voiced, nasal**. Compared with /m/, the phoneme /n/ lacks the feature **labial**. Otherwise, the two are the same. It is therefore the presence or absence of the feature labial which separates /m/ from /n/. Any feature which distinguishes one phoneme from another is called a **distinctive**

feature. Since languages will, in general, have a different range of phonemes, the set of distinctive features will also tend to differ from language to language. In some cases, however, different languages are found to have the same features, but in different combinations.

This type of feature analysis makes the rules of any language much simpler to express. Suppose you had a language which dropped the phonemes /m/ /n/ and /ŋ/ at the end of a word under certain circumstances. It is simpler and clearer to write a rule which states that nasals are dropped at the end of a word than it is to name each phoneme separately. A group of sounds which share important features in common, such as the group of nasals, are known as a **natural class** of sounds.

Non-segmental phonemes

English phonemes are chunks or segments of sound, such as /b/ or /t/ or /e/. These are known as **segmental** phonemes. However, a number of languages have not only segmental phonemes, but non-segmental phonemes also.

In North Mandarin Chinese, for example, there are numerous words which are distinguished by differences in the rise and fall of tone, as in the following minimal pairs (Figure 13):

ma	——	(level tone)	mother
ma	/	(rising tone)	hemp
ma	∨/	(dipping tone)	horse
ma	——	(falling tone)	scold

Fig. 13

Tone languages have one advantageous by-product: the tones and rhythms of speech can be imitated by instruments other than the human voice. This is the basis of African talking drums (or more accurately, talking gongs), in which the drum beats reproduce the tones and rhythms of the language. However, because the drums are unable to reproduce the segmental phonemes, their messages work in a slightly different way from normal language. A single message may take several minutes to convey, even though it would have taken only a few seconds to give the information verbally. This is because whole phrases are utilized where ordinary language uses single words. Such a procedure is necessary in order to avoid confusion. For example, among the Lokele of the Upper Congo, the word for dog is *ngwa*, a single syllable spoken with a low tone. But because there are dozens of other single syllable words spoken with a low tone, the drum equivalent for 'dog' uses a whole phrase, meaning literally 'giant dog, little one that barks kpei kpei'. The 'tune' of this phrase is unlike that of any other drum phrase, and serves to distinguish the meaning 'dog' in the message.

Metrical phonology

Although English does not have tones, it possesses important non-segmental features—characteristics which exist alongside the phonemes. In particular, each word and group of words has its own rhythm, an interplay of stressed and unstressed syllables. This branch of phonology is relatively new, and is known as **metrical phonology**.

In the words in Figure 14, the most stressed syllables have the most stars, and the least stressed, the smallest number of stars (some people leave the least stressed syllable unstarred, which would lower the number of stars all along):

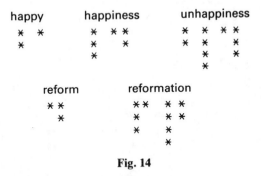

Fig. 14

The actual quantity of stress given to a syllable does not matter very much. The important point is the relative amount given to each. In *happiness*, for example, it is essential to give the greatest amount of stress to *hap-*, and the least to *-pi-*.

But this rhythm is not merely a sequence of different stress levels. It appears to have an internal structure, which can be represented on a 'tree diagram'—so-called because its branches resemble an upside-down tree. This shows the overall structure of the rhythm better than a grid of stars. It shows how strong and weak syllables alternate, and indicates that each syllable can be regarded as a sub-portion of a larger unit, sometimes called a **foot**. The words in Figure 15 have been split into a strong portion (S) and a weak portion (W), which in some cases is further subdivided:

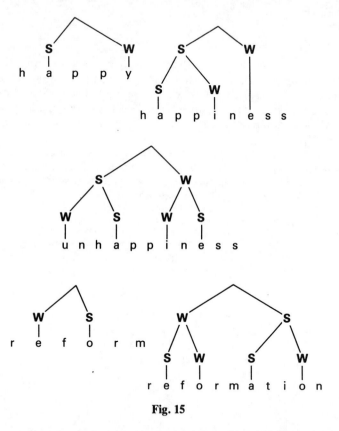

Fig. 15

The word rhythms outlined above are not static, in that they may change as words come into contact with one another. The words *central* and *heating* each sound rather similar when pronounced alone. But when spoken together as the phrase *central heating*, the rhythm alters, so that the strongest stress goes onto *heating* (Figure 16).

Fig. 16

QUESTIONS

1 What do you understand by the term **phoneme**?
2 What is a **minimal pair**? Suggest at least ten examples of minimal pairs in English.
3 What is an **allophone**? Give examples.
4 What are **distinctive features**?
5 What is a **natural class**?
6 What is **metrical phonology**?

6

Words and Pieces of Words

The **word** appears to be a widespread concept. Even in primitive cultures, informants are often able to identify words. This is somewhat surprising, because nobody has yet proposed a satisfactory universal definition of the notion 'word', or provided a foolproof method of identification. People sometimes wrongly assume that a word is recognizable because it represents a 'single piece of meaning'. But it can easily be shown that this view is wrong by looking at the lack of correspondence between words from different languages. In English, the three words *cycle repair outfit* correspond to one in German, *Fahrradreparaturwerkzeuge*. Or the six words *He used to live in Rome* are translated by two in Latin, *Romae habitabat*. And even in English, a word such as *walked* includes at least two 'pieces of meaning', 'walk' and 'past tense'.

This chapter will deal with this matter. First, it will look at the problems of defining and identifying **words**. Second, it will consider pieces of words, or **morphemes**.

Defining words

The best-known definition of a word is that proposed by the American linguist Bloomfield, who defined it as a *minimum free form*, that is, the smallest form that can occur by itself. This is fairly unsatisfactory, because words do not normally occur by themselves in spoken speech. Even if you ask a simple question, a normal-sounding reply often requires more than one word:

| *Who did that?* | *John did.* |
| *What's that?* | *An oak tree.* |

Furthermore, some apparent words, such as *did*, *the*, *and*, are found alone only in exceptional circumstances, such as in answer to the question: 'What does *a-n-d* spell?'

Bloomfield's definition works best for written English, where we conventionally leave a space on either side. But linguists are concerned primarily with the spoken word, not the written, and the two do not necessarily coincide. For example, it seems to be purely accidental that the name of a certain type of snake, a *boa constrictor*, is written as two words rather than one, or that *seaside* appears as one word, but *sea shore* as two.

Why have linguists found it so hard to find a satisfactory definition of the notion 'word'? The answer seems to be that there are different types of word. Consider the rhyme:

A flea and a fly in a flue
Were imprisoned, so what could they do?
Said the flea: 'Let us fly'.
Said the fly: 'Let us flee'.
So they flew through a flaw in the flue.

At the simplest level, this rhyme contains 36 written words. But some of these are repeated. If we decide to leave out repeats and count the number of different words, (in technical terms, count **word types** instead of **word tokens**), we come up against several problems. Should *fly* (noun) and *fly* (verb) be counted as the same, since they sound the same, or as different, because they have different meanings? Should *fly* and *flew* be regarded as the same, because they belong to the same verb, or as different because they have different forms? These problems can be solved only if we decide what kind of 'word' we are talking about. It is important to distinguish between **lexical items**, **syntactic words** and **phonological words**.

If by 'word' we mean **lexical item** (the technical term for 'dictionary entry'), then the sound sequence /flai/ 'fly' represents two words, since most dictionaries have separate entries for *fly* (noun) and *fly* (verb):

fly N: an insect with two wings.
fly V: to move through the air in a controlled manner.

This is perhaps the most basic, and most abstract use of the word 'word'. However, both of these lexical items have various syntactic forms associated with them. The insect could occur as *fly* (singular) or *flies* (plural), and the verb could occur as *fly*, *flies*, *flew*, *flown*. So if we counted the various syntactic forms as different words, the overall total would be much higher (Figure 17).

Lexical Items	Syntactic Words
fly N	fly
	flies
fly V	fly
	flies
	flew
	flown

Fig. 17

A further complication occurs with a lexical item such as *flaw*. This has the two syntactic forms *flaw* (singular) and *flaws* (plural). But the singular form *flaw* then has two different sound sequences associated with it, /flɔː/ before a consonant, and /flɔːr/ before a vowel (Figure 18):

*The flue had a **flaw** /flɔː/ which allowed the fly to escape.*
*There was a **flaw** /flɔːr/ in the flue.*

Lexical Items	Syntactic Words	Phonological Words
flaw N	flaw	/flɔː/
		/flɔːr/
	flaws	/flɔːz/

Fig. 18

These examples show that we must not expect an exact overlap between different types of word. And in some other languages, the situation is far more complex than in English. In Latin, for example, the lexical item *rosa* 'rose' has twelve different syntactic forms. In Welsh, the initial consonant of each word varies systematically, depending on the preceding sound: the word for 'father' could be *tad*, *dad*, *thad*, or *nhad*. The last lines of the chorus in a well-known Welsh hymn have three different forms of the verb meaning 'sing': *canu*, *ganu* and *chanu*—and there is a fourth possibility, *nghanu*, which the hymn omits.

Identifying words

For anyone working on an unknown language, it is important to identify these various types of word. There are two main stages in the analysis. First, finding chunks such as *fly*, *flew* which seem to recur as self-contained units. Second, deciding how many lexical items are covered by each chunk (as with *fly* which covers two lexical items), and conversely, deciding how many different chunks belong to the same lexical item (as with *fly*, *flew*, where different syntactic forms belong to one lexical item).

For the first stage, finding chunks which behave as self-contained units, we look for sequences which are uninterruptable and mobile. These are useful guidelines in many languages. A sequence such as *chickens* cannot be interrupted. It is impossible to say *chick-little-ens, or *chicken-little-s. In addition, the sequence *chickens* can move about. It can occur next to different words, and in different parts of the sentence, as in *Chickens lay eggs*, *Foxes eat chickens*, *The chickens clucked loudly*, and so on.

To take another example, suppose we had come across the sequence *greentrousers*, and wanted to know whether this was one or more words. We would begin by looking for sentences which included any part of the sequence *greentrousers*. We might find:

Green leather trousers.
Red trousers.
Green shirts.

The fact that *green trousers* can be interrupted by the word *leather* indicates that we are probably dealing with at least two words, *green* and *trousers*. This suspicion is confirmed by noting that both *green* and *trousers* occur with other words. But since *green* and *trousers* seem to be uninterruptible (we do not find *trous-green-ers, for example), we surmise that each is a word.

At the end of this stage of the analysis, we have a rough list of 'words', though a list in which we are likely to have clumped together different lexical items which sound the same (**homonyms**), and to have separated different syntactic forms of the same lexical item.

For the second stage of the analysis, we need to consider the syntactic behaviour of these possible 'words', that is, their role in the overall sentence pattern. For example, *fly* N would show up as behaving differently from *fly* V, since each would fit into a different 'slot' in the sentence:

The fly buzzed.
Birds fly.

On the other hand, *fly* and *flew* would turn out to be somewhat similar, in that they would fit into the same general slot:

They fly home on Sunday.
They flew home on Sunday.

However, the syntactic behaviour of these different forms can be supplemented by an analysis of their make-up, or, in other words, the **morphemes** out of which they are constituted. Let us therefore go on to consider some basic facets of **morphology**.

Morphemes

The smallest syntactic unit is the **morpheme**. Morphemes vary in size. Neither syllables nor length are any guide to their identification. The essential criterion is that a morpheme cannot be cut up into smaller syntactic segments.

The sentence in Figure 19 has eleven morphemes:

The	sleep	walk	ing	albatross	chant	ed	a	dream	y	lullaby
1	2	3	4	5	6	7	8	9	10	11

Fig. 19

The, *albatross*, *a*, *lullaby*, are all single morphemes because none of them can be syntactically split up further. *Alba-* and *-tross*, for example, do not have any other role to play in the syntax of English: they exist only as part of the single unit, *albatross*. *Chanted* and *dreamy*, on the other hand, each consist of two morphemes: *chant* is found in words such as *chanting, chants*, and is also a word by itself, while *-ed* is found in *wanted*, *batted* and so on. Similarly, *sleep-walking* consists of three morphemes, because *sleep*, *walk* and *-ing* are all found elsewhere. In theory there is no upper limit to the number of morphemes per word: *antidisestablishmentarianism*, for example, has at least six: *anti-dis-establish-ment-arian-ism*.

Recognition of morphemes

Linguists identify morphemes by comparing a wide variety of utterances. They look for utterances which are partially the same (Figure 20):

The	dinosaur	sniff-**ed**	arrogant-**ly**	and	plodd-**ed**	for-**wards**
The	dinosaur	grunt-**ed**	loud-**ly**	and	edg-**ed**	back-**wards**

Fig. 20

The partial similarity between *sniffed, grunted, plodded* and *edged* enables us to isolate the segment *-ed*. And the partial similarity between *arrogantly* and *loudly*, and between *backwards* and *forwards* makes it possible to isolate *-ly* and *-wards*.

In Turkish, the similarity between *adamlar*, 'men', and *kadınlar*, 'women', enables one to identify a plural suffix *-lar*, and the words for 'man', *adam*, and 'woman', *kadın*. In Swahili, the overlap between

nitasoma I will read
nilisoma I read (*past*)
utasoma you will read
ulisoma you read (*past*)

allows us to identify *soma*, 'read'; *ni*, 'I'; *u*, 'you'; *ta*, future tense; *li*, past tense.

Not all morphemes are as easily segmentable as these examples. But the identification of morphemes is done wholly by means of this one basic technique—the comparison of partially similar utterances.

Types of morpheme

Morphemes such as *albatross, chant, lullaby* which can occur by themselves as whole words are known as **free** morphemes. Those such as *anti-, -ed, -ly*, which must be attached to another, are **bound** morphemes.

Bound morphemes are of two main types. Consider the sentence:

*The owl **look-ed** up at the **cloud-y** sky.*

Superficially, both *looked* and *cloudy* have a similar make-up, consisting of one free morpheme, followed by a bound one. Yet the bound morphemes differ in nature. *-ed* on the end of *looked* is an *inflectional* morpheme, since it provides further information about an existing lexical item *look*, in this case indicating that the looking occurred in the past. Other examples of inflectional morphemes are the plural, as in *owls*, and the possessive, as in *Peter's car*. However,

-y on the end of *cloudy* behaves rather differently. It is a **derivational** morpheme, one which creates an entirely new word. *Cloud* and *cloudy* behave quite differently and fit into different slots in the sentence. Other examples of derivational morphemes are *-ness* as in *happiness*, *-ish* as in *greenish*, and *-ment* as in *establishment*.

In most cases, it is easy to tell the difference between inflection and derivation. Above all, inflectional endings do not alter the syntactic behaviour of an item in any major way. The word still fits into the same 'slot' in the sentence. Derivational endings create entirely new words. In addition, inflectional endings can be added on to derivational ones, but not vice-versa. That is, we find words such as *establish-ment-s*, but not *establish-s-ment*.

English has relatively few inflectional morphemes. These are on the whole easy to identify, though they sometimes present problems of analysis, as discussed below.

Allomorphs

Sometimes a morpheme has only one phonological form. But frequently it has a number of variants known as **allomorphs**.

Allomorphs may vary considerably. Totally dissimilar forms may be allomorphs of the same morpheme. *Cats*, *dogs*, *horses*, *sheep*, *oxen*, *geese* all contain the English plural morpheme.

An allomorph is said to be **phonologically conditioned** when its form is dependent on the adjacent phonemes. An allomorph is said to be **lexically conditioned** when its form seems to be a purely accidental one, linked to a particular vocabulary item.

The English plural morpheme provides excellent examples of both phonologically and lexically conditioned allomorphs. Let us look at some of these.

Phonological conditioning
The study of the different phonemic shapes of allomorphs is known as **morphophonology**—sometimes abbreviated to **morphonology**.

/-z/ /-s/ /-ɪz/ are all phonologically conditioned allomorphs of the English plural morpheme. That is, each allomorph occurs in a predictable set of environments:

/-z/ occurs after most voiced phonemes as in *dogs*, *lambs*, *bees*. (A voiced phoneme is one in which the vocal cords vibrate, as in /b/, /d/, /g/, /v/, and vowels.)

/-s/ occurs after most voiceless phonemes, as in *cats*, *giraffes*, *skunks*. (A voiceless phoneme is one in which the vocal cords do not vibrate.)

/-ɪz/ occurs after sibilants (hissing and hushing sounds), as in *horses, cheeses, dishes*.

If we take /z/ as basic, then we can express the distribution of these allomorphs by saying first, that /-z/ turns into /-ɪz/ after sibilants (Figure 21), and second, into /-s/ after voiceless sounds (Figure 22):

ø → ɪ/[+ sibilant] ——— z. e.g. /hɔːsz/ → /hɔːsɪz/

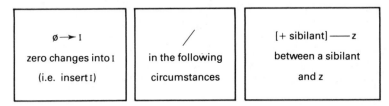

Fig. 21

z → s/[—voice] ———. e.g. /kætz/ → /kæts/

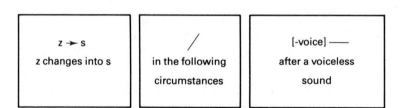

Fig. 22

Note that these 'rules' must be applied in the order given above. If the order was reversed, we would get forms such as ⋆[dɪʃs] instead of the correct [dɪʃɪz] for the plural of *dish*.

Lexical conditioning

Words such as *oxen, sheep, geese* present a problem. Although they function as plurals in the same way as *cats, dogs*, they are not marked as plurals in the same way. Such lexically conditioned plurals do not follow any specific rule. Each one has to be learnt separately.

Words such as *oxen, sheep, geese* can be identified as syntactically equivalent to the *cats* and *dogs* type of plural because they fit into the same 'slot' in a sentence (Figure 23):

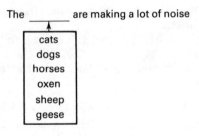

Fig. 23

Oxen, *sheep* and *geese* each contain two morphemes:

> *ox* + plural
> *sheep* + plural
> *goose* + plural

But only *oxen* is easily divisible into two:

> *ox* + /-ən/ (*-en*)

Sheep can be divided into two if a **zero suffix** is assumed. A 'zero suffix' is a convenient linguistic fiction which is sometimes used in cases of this type. It is normally written /ø/:

> *sheep* + /ø/.

There is no obvious way to analyse *geese*. At one time, linguists suggested that the plural vowel /iː/ in /giːs/ (*geese*) which replaces the /uː/ in /guːs/ (*goose*) should be regarded as a special type of allomorph called a **replacive**. And they analysed the plural as:

> /guːs/ + /iː/ ← (/uː/).

Here the formula /iː/ ←(/uː/) means '/iː/ replaces /uː/'.

But this is rather a strained explanation. These days, most linguists simply accept that the form /giːs/ (*geese*) represents two morphemes,

> *goose* + plural

and that these two cannot be separated. And a similar explanation is required for forms such as *went*, *took*, which represent

> *go* + past tense
> *take* + past tense.

Word classes

In every language, there are a limited number of types of lexical item. These different kinds of word are traditionally known as 'parts of speech', though in linguistic terminology the label **word class** is more common. Word classes are conventionally given labels, such as noun, verb, adjective.

Words are classified into word classes partly on account of their syntactic behaviour, partly on the basis of their morphological form. That is, words from the same word class are likely to fit into the same slot in a sentence, and to be inflected in similar ways. For example, the word class traditionally known as 'verb' can be recognized as a verb partly because it occurs after nouns (or phrases containing a noun), and partly because most verbs have an inflectional ending *-ed* to indicate the past:

*Arabella **detested** snails.*
*Marianna **smiled**.*

Careful analysis is needed, because in some cases, items which superficially appear to fit into the same slot in a sentence can turn out to be rather different in character. Consider the sentences:

*Charlie ate **caviare**.*
*Charlie ate **well**.*

At first sight, we might wrongly assume that *caviare* and *well* belong to the same word class. But a less superficial analysis reveals that they behave somewhat differently overall. If we tried altering the sentences around, we could say:

Caviare was eaten by Charlie.
What Charlie ate was caviare.

But we could not form the equivalent sentences with *well*:

*Well was eaten by Charlie.
*What Charlie ate was well.

These dissimilarities indicate that *caviare* and *well* are syntactically different, and belong to different word classes.

It is not always easy to tell how many word classes a language contains. Many traditional textbooks claim that English has eight 'parts of speech'. But this claim turns out to be based largely on old Latin grammars which were in turn translated from ancient Greek grammars, which mostly divided Greek words into eight word classes. If we look more closely, we find several discrepancies. For example, nouns and pronouns are traditionally classified as separate parts of speech, yet they have a large number of similarities:

Max *laughed.*
He *laughed.*

In fact, nouns and pronouns are more alike than the different types of word which are traditionally labelled adverbs. Words such as *quickly* and *very* are both usually classified as adverbs, but they behave quite differently:

He ran **quickly**.
*He ran **very**.

The number of word classes varies from language to language. Some word classes, such as noun and verb, may be universal. But others vary. In some languages, for example, there is no distinct class of adjectives. Where English says:

Petronella is happy.

a language such as Chinese might say, as it were:

Petronella happies.

using a verb instead of an adjective.

Major word classes

English is sometimes considered to have four major word classes: noun (N), adjective (A), verb (V), preposition (P) (Figure 24), as well as a number of minor ones, such as determiner (D) which covers words such as *the*, *a*, *this*, *that*.

Big	frogs	swim	under	water
A	N	V	P	N

Fig. 24

Of these four major classes, nouns, verbs and prepositions behave fairly differently from one another, though adjectives are somewhat strange, in that they have some noun-like qualities, and some verb-like ones. In *Blessed are the* **brave**, *brave* seems to have become a noun. And in *Mavis is* **asleep**, *asleep* seems fairly verb-like, since it fits into the same slot as *sleeping* in a sentence such as *Mavis is sleeping*.

It has been suggested that we should describe these four word classes in a manner parallel to the distinctive feature descriptions used for sounds, which can show shared similarities:

Noun	$[+N, -V]$
Verb	$[-N, +V]$
Adjective	$[+N, +V]$
Preposition	$[-N, -V]$

Although not yet generally accepted, this seems to be a useful and economical way of capturing the similarities and differences between the major word classes.

QUESTIONS

1 Suggest three different ways in which the word **word** might be used.
2 What is a **morpheme**?
3 Distinguish between **inflection** and **derivation**.
4 What is the difference between **phonologically conditioned allomorphs** and **lexically conditioned allomorphs**?
5 How might one identify **word classes**?

7

Sentence Patterns

Words by themselves, or words strung together in a random way, are of relatively little use, a fact known by anyone who has visited a foreign country armed only with a dictionary, and no knowledge of the language. Does *me - bus* mean 'I am a bus', 'A bus hit me', 'I came by bus', or 'I want to go by bus'? So let us now look at how words may be combined together into longer utterances.

In this chapter, we shall consider, first, the ways in which words may be linked together to form larger units. Second, we shall discuss how to analyse sentences into their component parts, or **constituents** in linguistic terminology. Third, we shall suggest ways of representing this analysis.

Linking words together

Different languages use different devices for showing the relationship of one word to another. Most languages have one or two favourite devices. The following are especially common.

Word order

The device used most frequently in English is **word order**:

The large spider frightened Aunt Matilda.
Aunt Matilda frightened the large spider.

The words themselves in these two sentences are identical. It is the word order which indicates who frightened whom, and that it is the spider which is large, not Aunt Matilda. Languages which rely heavily on word order are known as **configurational** languages.

Inflections

In a language such as Latin, word endings or **inflections**, indicate the relationship between words. In the sentence:

Magna aranea perterruit Matildam amitam.
(Large-spider-frightened-Matilda - aunt)
'The large spider frightened Aunt Matilda'.

the word order is irrelevant. The sentence would still mean the same if the words were arranged quite differently as in:

Magna Matildam perterruit amitam aranea.
(Large-Matilda-frightened - Aunt - spider)

The endings alone show that it was the spider which terrified Aunt Matilda, not the reverse, and that it is the spider, not Aunt Matilda, which is large.

Function words

Another common device, used to some extent in both English and Latin, is the use of **function words**. These are the so-called 'empty words', such as *of*, *by*, which often exist solely to indicate syntactic relationships, and do not normally refer to identifiable objects, qualities, or actions in the external world:

*Aunt Matilda was terrified **by** a spider.*
*The Queen **of** Sheba.*
*Matilda amita **ab** aranea perterrita est.*
(Matilda-aunt-**by**-spider-frightened-is[was])

Constituent analysis

Sentences are not simply random words strung together by means of various devices. We do not find English sentences such as:

**The large spider terrified Aunt Matilda swims of Sheba by a car.*

Instead, English (like every other language) has a limited number of recurring sentence patterns. A fundamental technique of syntactic analysis is to identify these patterns by a process of successive substitution. Take the sentence:

The duck bit the burglar.

In this sentence, *the* and *duck* can be replaced by a single word such as *Donald*, *it*, without altering the basic sentence pattern. This suggests that these two words are closely linked, and together constitute a single, larger component. Similarly, the words *the* and *burglar* go together, since they also could be replaced by a word such as *Albert*, *him*. So as a first stage, we have reduced a sentence with five original components down to three more basic ones (Figure 25):

Fig. 25

Of these three components, the final two could be replaced by a single word such as *slept*. We therefore conclude that they could be bracketed together as a single, larger component. We have therefore reduced a sentence with five components down to a basic two (Figure 26):

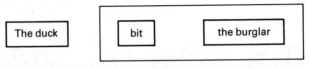

Fig. 26

The linguistic procedure which divides sentences into their component parts or constituents in this way is known as **constituent analysis**. The test of substitution is basic to such an analysis, though the process is not always as straightforward as the example above.

Tree diagrams

The successive layers of constituents which make up a sentence can be shown most clearly on a **tree diagram**—so called because its branches resemble the branches of a tree. In a tree diagram, a basic sentence type at the top branches downwards in ever-increasing complexity (Figure 27).

Fig. 27

The advantage of a tree diagram is that each join or **node** on the tree can be labelled, so that the whole construction becomes clearer (Figure 28).

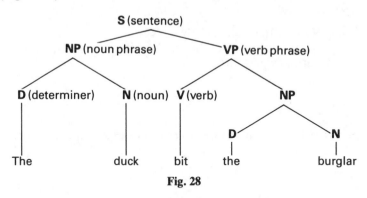

Fig. 28

A family metaphor is used to refer to the relationships on a tree (Figure 29). A higher node is a **mother**, and the nodes on the branches immediately beneath her are her **daughters**. Daughters of the same mother are known as **sisters**. A mother is said to **dominate** the nodes beneath her. She **immediately dominates** her daughters, but she also dominates her granddaughters, and great-granddaughters, as it were.

Fig. 29

Rewrite rules

An alternative way of expressing the information found on a tree diagram is by means of **rewrite** rules. A rewrite rule is a replacement rule, in which the symbol to the left of an arrow is replaced by an expanded form written to the right of the arrow:

S → NP   VP

means 'Replace the symbol S by NP VP'.

VP → V   NP

means 'Replace the symbol VP by V NP'.

NP → D   N

means 'Replace the symbol NP by D N'.

The essential structure of *The duck bit the burglar* can therefore be summarised in just three rules:

    S → NP   VP
    VP → V   NP
    NP → D   N

On a tree diagram, these three rules would appear as in Figure 30.

Fig. 30

These branching rules can then be supplemented by lexical substitution rules:

N → *duck*, *burglar*
V → *bit*
D → *the*

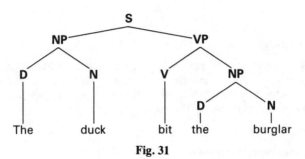

Fig. 31

The great advantage of rewrite rules is that they are perfectly **explicit**. They do not leave anything to the imagination. By following them, you could produce a perfect English sentence even if you did not know any English, since the rules are applied mechanically, step-by-step, one symbol at a time.

Note, however, that the above rewrite rules could also have resulted in the sentence:

The burglar bit the duck.

This does not matter, as the sequence is a perfectly good sentence of English (though admittedly a somewhat unlikely one). The rewrite rules are there to tell us what is a well-formed English sentence, not to give us information about the probable behaviour of burglars.

Identifying constituents

As we have seen, every sentence can be broken down into successive layers of constituents. However, not all sentences can be analysed with as little trouble as *The duck bit the burglar.* Consider the sentence:

The mouse ran up the clock.

How should this be analysed? Should we bracket [*ran up*] together, on the assumption that these words could be replaced by a word such as *climbed*? Or should we bracket [*up the clock*] together, noting that the whole phrase could be replaced by a single word such as *upwards*? Problems of this type are solved by seeing whether the groups of words in question belong together as a constituent elsewhere, since words that are grouped together as a unit in one sentence are likely to recur as a single constituent in other sentences. One way of checking this is to construct sentences in which the original words occur in a different order:

Up the clock ran the mouse.
*The mouse ran the clock up.

These sentences suggest that the words *up the clock* should be regarded as a unit, since when the original sentence is switched around, the new sentence is well-formed when the words *up the clock* remain together, but ill-formed when they are separated. We may therefore analyse the sentence as

[*The mouse*]   [*ran*]   [*up the clock.*]

and draw the tree diagram as in Figure 32 (page 74).

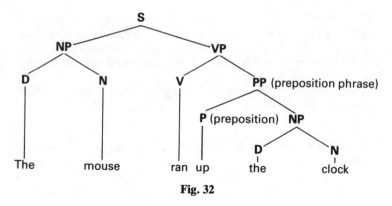

Fig. 32

The sentence discussed above must be analysed differently from another, superficially similar sentence:

The mouse ate up the cheese.

We can show the difference by switching the sentence around:

★*Up the cheese ate the mouse.*
(Compare: *Up the clock ran the mouse.*)
The mouse ate the cheese up.
(Compare: ★*The mouse ran the clock up.*)

We may therefore analyse the second sentence as:

[*The mouse*]   [*ate up*]   [*the cheese.*]

and draw the tree diagram as in Figure 33, using the extra node-labels VB for 'phrasal verb' and PRT for 'particle':

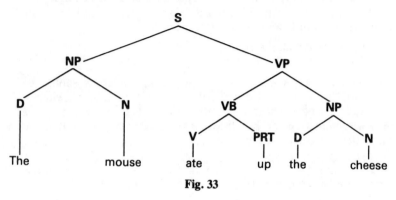

Fig. 33

NP tests

Since languages ring the changes on a few recurring patterns, constituents behave in predictable ways. It is therefore possible to apply specific 'tests' for the presence of a particular constituent in a given language. English NPs, for example, recur in certain specifiable positions. Some of the main places in which they occur are:

(*a*)   At the beginning of a sentence before the verb:
The cat *ate the canary.*

(*b*)   At the end of a sentence after the verb:
The canary feared **the cat**.

(*c*)   After *by* in a passive sentence:
The canary was eaten by **the cat**.

(*d*)   After an auxiliary verb in questions:
Did **the cat** *eat the canary?*

Consequently, if we find a phrase which we suspect might be an NP, we can apply these (and other) tests. For example, consider the sentences below:

Uncle Harry kicked the cat.
Suddenly Harry kicked the cat.

In order to find out whether the first two words in each sentence are NPs, we can apply the NP tests listed above:

(*a*)   At the beginning of a sentence before a verb:
Uncle Harry *kicked the cat.*
Suddenly Harry *kicked the cat.*

(*b*)   At the end of a sentence after a verb:
The cat scratched **Uncle Harry**.
★The cat scratched **suddenly Harry**.

(*c*)   After *by* in a passive sentence:
The cat was kicked by **Uncle Harry**.
★The cat was kicked by **suddenly Harry**.

(*d*)   After an auxiliary verb in questions:
Did **Uncle Harry** *kick the cat?*
★Did **suddenly Harry** *kick the cat?*

The failure of *suddenly Harry* to pass most of these NP tests shows that it cannot be an NP, whereas the success of *Uncle Harry* indicates that it probably is an NP.

Adding in extra patterns

So far, our rewrite rules have dealt with only one structure, the pattern underlying *The duck bit the burglar*. Let us now add in some others. Consider the sentence:

The duck slept in the bath.

This has the same basic division into NP VP as *The duck bit the burglar*. But the structure of the VP differs. In *The duck slept in the bath*, the verb is followed by a preposition phrase (PP) (Figure 34).

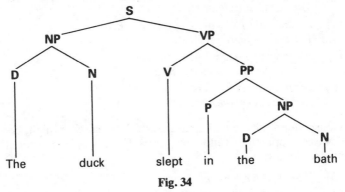

Fig. 34

The extra rewrite rules required for this are:

   VP → V   PP
   PP → P   NP

However, the PP is not an essential part of the structure. It is an optional extra, since *The duck slept* is a well-formed sentence by itself. This can be shown by putting brackets round the PP in the rewrite rule, indicating that it is optional:

   VP → V   (PP)

The rewrite rule above therefore underlies both *The duck slept in the bath*, and *The duck slept*. In the first, the optional PP has been selected. In the second, it has been omitted.

Let us now consider another sentence:

The burglar put the duck in a sack.

This differs from the previous structures discussed in that it is essential to have both an NP and a PP after the V (Figure 35). If either were omitted, the sentence would be ill-formed:

The burglar put the duck.
The burglar put in a sack.

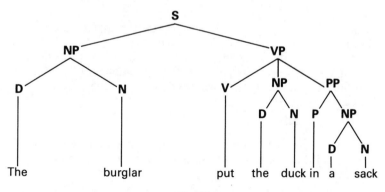

Fig. 35

The rewrite rule in this case is:

VP → V   NP   PP

So far, then, we have three different rewrite rules for English VPs:

VP → V   NP   (*The duck bit the burglar*).
VP → V   (PP)   (*The duck slept, The duck slept in the bath*).
VP → V   NP   PP   (*The burglar put the duck in a sack*).

It would be useful to combine these three separate rules. As a first suggestion, one might simply number the types of verb (V1 for a verb such as *bit*, V2 for *slept*, V3 for *put*), and enclose them in another type of bracket { } which is used to denote alternative possibilities:

$$VP \rightarrow \begin{Bmatrix} V1 & NP \\ V2 & (PP) \\ V3 & NP & PP \end{Bmatrix}$$

This means: 'Rewrite the VP as either V1 NP, or V2 (PP), or V3 NP PP'. However, if we wanted to include the full range of alternatives available in an English VP, the rewrite rules would become extremely long and complicated. A neater solution is to keep the rewrite rules fairly simple, and to use them in conjunction with a lexicon (dictionary) which specifies the structure associated with each V:

```
bit    V   [—NP]
slept  V   [—(PP)]
put    V   [—NP PP]
```

First, the item in question is listed, then the fact that it is a verb (V). In the square brackets come the structures associated with it. The long dash [—] indicates the place where the verb is inserted, so [—NP] says 'The verb in question must be followed by an NP'.

With these lexical entries, we need only one rewrite rule for the three types of verb:

VP → V   (NP)   (PP)

This rule says: 'A VP consists of a V optionally followed by an NP and/or a PP'. It accounts for all the possibilities discussed above, since one can slot in a verb only if it fits the structure chosen. For example, suppose we had chosen both the optional items, NP and PP, we must then slot in a verb followed by NP PP, in this case *put*. Similarly, if we had chosen V alone, the only V which fits in this case is *sleep*.

With a detailed lexicon of this type, which can be expanded to include other word classes also, we no longer need substitution rules such as: V → *bit*, N → *burglar*.

Let us therefore summarize the rewrite rules and lexical entries for:

The duck bit the burglar.
The duck slept.
The duck slept in the bath.
The burglar put the duck in a sack.

A   Rewrite rules

```
S    → NP   VP
VP   → V   (NP)   (PP)
NP   → D   N
PP   → P   NP
```

B   Lexicon

```
burglar   N
duck      N
sack      N
bath      N
bit       V   [—NP]
```

slept	V	[—(PP)]
put	V	[—NP PP]
the	D	
a	D	
in	P	

Of course, if more data had been considered, the rules and the lexicon would have to be complicated further. For example, if we had included a proper name such as *Donald*, the lexicon would have to specify which nouns are found with a determiner (D), as in *the duck*, *a sack*, and which not, as in *Donald* not *a Donald*. However, we set out to write rules for the sentence patterns in question, and we have done this as economically as possible.

Layers of branches

The tree diagrams we have considered so far have relatively few layers. But consider a sentence such as:

Maurice took a photograph of a platypus.

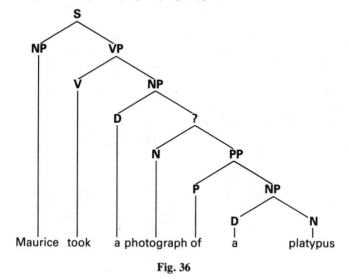

Fig. 36

The sequence *a photograph of a platypus* is clearly a noun phrase (NP) and the words *photograph* and *platypus* are nouns (N). But what of the intervening node, comprising *photograph of a platypus*?

It seems to be something between an N and a full NP, so what is it? A useful solution is to give the label N̄ (pronounced N-bar, since it has a bar along the top) to something that is neither a simple N, nor a whole NP. Some people also give the label N̄̄ (N-double bar) to a whole NP. (In Figure 37, a triangle has been drawn in place of the details of the PP. This is a standard procedure which avoids wasting time and space when the details are irrelevant to the point under discussion.)

Fig. 37

The use of bars has one further major advantage: they can be used with adjectives (A), verbs (V), and prepositions (P), as well as with nouns (N). It is then easy to see similarities in structure between NPs, APs (adjective phrases), VPs and PPs which were not so evident before. It turns out that the **head** (main word) in one type of phrase is in a very similar position to the head in another. In other words, a noun in an NP is likely to be in a parallel location to an adjective in an AP, a verb in a VP and a preposition in a PP. For

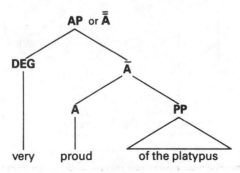

Fig. 38

example, the AP *very proud of the platypus* has a structure that is similar in its branching pattern to the NP *a photograph of the platypus.* (In Figure 38, DEG stands for 'degree').

A number of details still have to be worked out concerning **X-bar syntax** or **X-bar theory**, the name of this method of dealing with sentence patterns. For example, there is some controversy as to how many layers of bars it is useful to set up. But the theory appears to be here to stay, and it plays an important role in Chomsky's latest theories (Chapter 16).

Complex sentences

So far, we have assumed that all sentences are simple ones such as

The duck bit the burglar.
The mouse ran up the clock.

In practice, however, many sentences have one or more sentence-like structures attached to them or inserted inside them. Anyone analysing sentences must be able to recognize such structures. Consider the sentence:

Archibald played tennis, and Peter went fishing.

Here we have two sub-sentences of equal importance attached together to form a single one. This process is known as **conjoining**. In theory an indefinite number of sentences could be joined together:

Archibald played tennis, and Peter went fishing, and Pip played cricket, and Mary washed her hair, and Drusilla climbed the Eiffel tower . . .

and so on.

However, conjoining is not the only process by which sentence-like structures are linked together. More often subsidiary sentences are inserted into one main sentence. This is known as **embedding** (Figure 39):

The rumour that the dinosaur had escaped worried the public.

Fig. 39

In theory, a sentence can have an indefinite number of sentences embedded in it. In *The fact that the rumour that the dinosaur had escaped worried the public is not surprising*, the simple sentence has two others embedded in it (Figure 40):

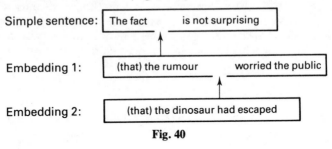

Fig. 40

Another example of embedding is the old nursery rhyme (Figure 41):

Fig. 41

Both embedding and conjoining illustrate an important property of language—that of **recursion**.

Recursion is the possibility of repeatedly re-using the same construction, so that there is no fixed limit to the length of sentences. This has important implications. It means that we can never make a complete list of all the possible sentences of any language. Instead, we must work out the system of rules which underlie the sentences.

It is quite easy to incorporate recursion into the rewrite rules, if one allows a symbol such as VP to be rewritten to include an S:

VP → V   S

This rule (which would need to be combined with the other VP rule discussed earlier) allows one to generate a sentence such as:

Mavis believes the burglar took the duck.

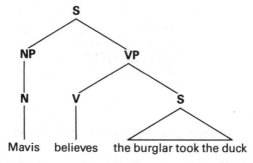

Fig. 42

QUESTIONS

1   Suggest three ways in which languages show the relationship of one word to another.
2   What is a **tree diagram**, and why is it useful?
3   What are **rewrite rules**?
4   Draw a tree diagram and formulate rewrite rules for the sentence:
    The monkey put the coconut in a hole.
5   Draw a tree diagram for each of the following sentences:
    The bus ran down the dog.
    The boy ran down the street.
6   Distinguish between **conjoining** and **embedding**. Give examples.

8

Meaning

The study of meaning is normally referred to as 'semantics', from the Greek noun *sema*, 'sign, signal', and the verb *semaino* 'signal, mean'. A linguist who is studying meaning tries to understand why certain words and constructions can be combined together in a semantically acceptable way, while others cannot. For example, it is quite all right to say:

My brother is a bachelor.
The camel sniffed the chocolate and then ate it.
The platypus remained alive for an hour after the hunter shot it.
Socrates arrived yesterday.

but not:

⋆*My brother is a spinster.*
⋆*The camel swallowed the chocolate and then ate it.*
⋆*The platypus remained alive for an hour after the hunter killed it.*
⋆*Socrates arrived tomorrow.*

These sentences are all well-formed syntactically: nouns, verbs, and so on are all in the right order. But they are contradictory. An English hearer could interpret them only by assuming that the speaker has made a mistake, in which case he would say, for instance, 'A brother *can't* be a spinster, you must mean "bachelor"'.

A linguist studying semantics would also like to know why anyone who knows a language can recognize certain phrases and sentences as having similar meanings, and would ask how it is that people can recognize:

Indicate to me the route to my habitual abode,
I am fatigued and I wish to retire,

> *I imbibed a small amount of alcohol approximately 60 minutes*
> *   ago,*
> *And it has flowed into my cerebellum,*

as roughly equivalent to:

> *Show me the way to go home,*
> *I'm tired and I want to go to bed,*
> *I had a little drink about an hour ago,*
> *And it's gone right to my head.*

A further human ability which needs explaining is the fact that hearers not only recognize ambiguous sentences, but they can also use the surrounding context to choose the most likely of the possible interpretations. For example:

> *Visiting great-aunts can be a nuisance.*

is ambiguous. Are the great-aunts coming to see us, or are we going to see them? But if someone came across the sentence

> *Visiting great-aunts can be a nuisance: I wish we didn't have to go.*

he would have no doubt that we are visiting the great-aunts, rather than vice versa.

Word meaning

Clearly, the question of meaning is to a large extent connected with the meaning of individual words, or (more accurately) **lexical items**—since (as we saw in Chapter 6) the word 'word' can be misleading: *boa constrictor*, we noted, is two written words, but a single lexical item. So in a sentence such as:

> *⋆My brother is a spinster*

we need to find out about the meaning of *brother* and *spinster* in order to see why such a sequence is unacceptable.

Three preliminary points need to be clarified in connection with word meaning. First of all, we shall be concerned primarily with so-called 'full' words, such as *zoo, apple, jump, red*, rather than with 'empty' items such as *of, that, by, which* whose role is mainly to show the relationship between syntactic units (though the distinction between the two is not always clear-cut).

Second, we shall be dealing only with straightforward descriptive meaning, and ignoring what is sometimes called 'emotive' meaning or 'connotation'. For example, the word *adolescent* will be taken to mean someone who is between childhood and adulthood. We shall be ignoring the fact that some people use the word to imply that the person concerned is also likely to be awkward, immature, obstinate and moody.

Third, we must be aware that meaning is double-faced. The meaning of a lexical item such as *tree* must be considered in two ways: first of all, as one element in a language system, whose 'meaning' is dependent on relationships with the other words in the system. Second, its 'meaning' is linked up with a certain class of recognizable objects in the external world (Figure 43).

Fig. 43

Linguists regard these two aspects as complementary: they examine first one, then the other, starting with the **internal** relationships between linguistic elements.

As with all linguistic elements, every lexical item has its own particular place in the pattern. By studying the relationships of individual items, linguists can build up a picture of the overall structure of a language's vocabulary. When they do this they must forget that a word such as *apple* refers to an objectively identifiable object in the outside world, and must concentrate solely on its relationships with the other items in the language.

Semantic fields

Every language cuts up the world in different ways. It is not simply that one language sometimes has more subdivisions than another in certain areas (for example, Arabic has numerous words for different types of camel, where English has a variety of words for different types of dog). The situation is far more complicated. The set of words covering a certain area in one language is unlikely to correspond to those in any other language, even when the speakers share similar cultures. This is often illustrated by the field of colour terminology. For example, Welsh and English speakers have in the past led fairly similar lives, yet Welsh *glas* traditionally covers not only the area that English speakers would call blue, but also part of green and grey as well (Figure 44). Frequently nowadays the traditional colour boundaries tend to be confused with the English ones.

English	Welsh
green	gwyrdd
blue	glas
grey	llwyd

Fig. 44

Yet even colour terms reflect a spuriously simple situation, since the spectrum has well-defined boundaries. More usually, we are faced with a much messier state of affairs. For example, it is impossible to translate the sentence 'The cat sat on the mat' accurately into French without further information about the state of affairs described. We would have to decide arbitrarily whether the cat was sitting on a doormat (*paillasson*), a small rug (*tapis*), or a bedside mat (*descente de lit*). None of the French words corresponds exactly to our word 'mat' or 'rug' or 'carpet': *tapis* is often used to translate English 'carpet' as well as 'rug'.

These examples show us that for linguists, it is important to deal with the lexical structure of a language rather than with isolated words. The word *green* in English only becomes meaningful in relation to its neighbours in the set of colour terms: it denotes the colour between blue and yellow. Purple denotes the colour between red and blue. In semantics, as in phonology and syntax, language is not an accidental junk-heap consisting of a haphazard collection of different items. Instead, it is more like a jigsaw puzzle, where each piece fits into those which surround it, and where an isolated piece simply does not make sense if it is moved from its place in the overall pattern. We have a situation where,

> *'every word is at home*
> *Taking its place to support the others'.*
> (T. S. ELIOT)

In such a situation, it is useful to look at groups of lexical items which seem to belong together. Each item in a group or **set** can be defined by its place in relation to the other members of the set (Figure 45). *Adolescent* denotes someone who is no longer a child, but not yet an adult. *Cool* is the temperature between cold and warm. For many people, *copse* refers to an entity between a tree and a wood.

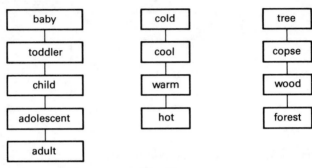

Fig. 45

Such a study can give a useful picture of the way in which a particular semantic area is divided up. It would be wrong, however, to assume that lexical items cover an entire field like a smooth mosaic. In fact, there are plenty of gaps and overlaps. In English, a gap is sometimes claimed to exist in the field of dead objects. We have a word *corpse* meaning 'body of dead human being' and *carcase* meaning 'body of dead animal', but no comparable word for a dead plant. But overlapping is perhaps the greatest problem. For example, *cow*, *princess* and *tigress* overlap in that they are all female. *Calf*, *puppy* and *baby* overlap in that they are all young and immature. *Murder*, *assassinate* and *execute* all involve the notion of killing. Let us consider how to deal with this type of problem.

Coping with overlaps

At one time, linguists hoped it might prove possible to split lexical items up into their component parts. Word meanings, like phonemes (Chapter 5), were assumed to be made up out of a stock of basic components. The word *bull* might consist of the components MALE/BOVINE/ADULT, as opposed to *cow* which would be FEMALE/BOVINE/ADULT, and *calf* which would be BOVINE/NON-

ADULT. The attempt to divide lexical items into component parts is known as **componential analysis**. It feels fairly familiar because dictionaries often perform a similar type of analysis in an informal manner. For example, in the *Concise Oxford Dictionary*, *mare* is defined as 'female of equine animal'.

Componential analysis, it was thought, accounted naturally for overlaps, since one could point to components which were apparently shared by overlapping words: *cow*, *princess* and *tigress* overlapped because they shared the component FEMALE. And this type of analysis could also be extended to verbs:

die	BECOME NOT ALIVE
kill	CAUSE BECOME NOT ALIVE
murder	INTENTIONALLY CAUSE HUMAN BEING BECOME NOT ALIVE
slaughter	INTENTIONALLY CAUSE ANIMATE BEING BECOME NOT ALIVE

Unfortunately, however, it is somewhat inaccurate to speak of the meaning of words as being 'composed' out of a heap of separate components. At best, these so-called components form only a small part of the overall meaning of the word in question, and the whole approach wrongly suggests that if we looked a little more carefully, we might be able to sort out all of them. The words 'component' and 'componential analysis' have therefore faded out of fashion. Nowadays, people tend to talk of words having 'semantic properties', which is somewhat more satisfactory, since it does not imply that these properties are 'building blocks' which need to be assembled.

Synonyms and opposites

To gain a fuller understanding of how lexical items hang together within a language, we need to look at the different types of relationship which exist between words. For example, the **synonyms** and **opposites** of a word can give valuable insights into its links with the rest of the vocabulary.

Lexical items can be regarded as synonymous if they can be interchanged without altering the meaning of an utterance:

*He **snapped** the twig in half.*
*He **broke** the twig in half.*

By studying interchangeable items, a linguist can build up a picture of those with similar meanings.

Note however that perfect synonymy is rare. That is, it is very unusual for two lexical items to have exactly the same meanings in all contexts. Occasionally, such synonymy is found between formal and informal vocabulary items. For example, *rubella* is the term found in medical literature for the disease that is more generally known as *German measles*. But, usually, a lexical item only partially overlaps another, and the two are synonymous only in certain contexts. To return to the words *snap* and *break*:

*He **snapped** his fingers.*

does not mean the same as

*He **broke** his fingers.*

And although

*He **broke** the record for the 100 metre sprint.*

is an acceptable sentence,

*He **snapped** the record for the 100 metre sprint.*

would seem unusual to most English speakers.

The study of opposites is more complex, as there are several different types of opposites. For this reason, the word 'antonym' has been avoided. Some writers use it for all types of opposite, others for one kind only.

The most obvious type is a pair of words in which the negative of one implies the other:

*He is not **married**: he is **single**
He is not **single**: he is **married**.*

A second type of opposite is one which is not absolute, but relative to some standard. *Small* and *large*, for example, always imply some comparison:

*What a **large** mouse!* (=what a large mouse in comparison to a normal-size mouse)
*What a **small** elephant!* (=what a small elephant in comparison to a normal-size elephant)

A third type is when one word is the converse of the other. The choice of one opposite rather than another depends on the angle from which you view the situation being described:

*I **give** you the book: you **take** the book.*

Classification (inclusion)

A further way of examining lexical structure is to note the ways in which a language classifies items. In English, for example, claret and hock are classified as 'wines'. Tea and coffee are referred to as 'beverages'. And wines and beverages both come under the heading of 'drinks'.

This indicates that the vocabulary of a language is partially hierarchically structured. In Figure 46 below, more general items come at the top, and more specific items are sub-divisions of these:

Fig. 46

The vocabulary of English is classified in this way in Roget's *Thesaurus*. Each entry has under it a list of **hyponyms** (i.e. lexical items subsumed under it). Its main drawback is that it does not distinguish between the stylistic or social variables which control the choice of synonyms.

The advantage of looking at these different relationships is firstly, they enable us to understand the multiple links between different words. Second, they can all be expressed by means of logical notation, so allowing us to be explicit in our description. Indeed, some linguists have claimed that the entire meaning of a word can be expressed in terms of its logical relationships with other words.

Fuzziness and family resemblances

So far, we have assumed that words have an agreed-upon meaning which we can discover and describe. But this is true only of some lexical items. For others, it seems to be impossible to agree upon a 'proper meaning'.

Consider the words *bachelor* and *tiger*. As a first step, we can look up these words in the *Concise Oxford Dictionary*. Here a *bachelor* is defined as an 'unmarried man'. Both unmarriedness and maleness seem to be essential properties of the word *bachelor*. If someone said, 'I met a bachelor and he was married', the automatic response would be 'Then he isn't a bachelor'. Or if someone said 'I know a girl who is a bachelor', the normal response would be, 'That's impossible' (unless they happened to be talking about someone who possessed a Bachelor of Arts degree). It is therefore clear that *bachelor* contains the properties *male/unmarried*. This word has proved easy to analyse.

Let us now look at the word *tiger*. A dictionary definition is 'large Asian yellow-brown black-striped carnivorous maneless feline'. Which of these are essential characteristics? Presumably 'carnivorous' is not really essential, because you could say, 'Harry's tiger is not carnivorous' without getting the response, 'That's impossible, it can't be a tiger'. But what about stripiness? Here people's reactions differ. If you said 'Harry's tiger isn't striped', people's reactions fall into two categories. Some might say, 'Then it's not a tiger', indicating that stripiness is an essential part of being a tiger. But others might make a comment such as 'Well I suppose you can get albino tigers just as you get albino blackbirds', or 'Since tabby cats don't always have tabby kittens, maybe you can get unstriped tigers'. To such people, stripiness is not an essential property of tigerhood.

In brief, with some words (such as *bachelor*), there is a relatively high level of agreement as to which properties constitute an essential part of their meaning, but with others (such as *tiger*), no such agreement is found.

Fuzziness is another problem. Words often have fuzzy edges. There is no absolute divide between a cup and a mug, a glass and a vase, or a plate and a saucer. They all merge into one another. People use them inconsistently, calling something a *vase* one day, and a *glass* the next. They might call it a *vase* if it held flowers, and a *glass* if it held orange-juice.

Family resemblances create further difficulties. Sometimes a word such as *furniture* covers a whole range of things, which share characteristics with one another, as do members of a family. Yet it may be impossible to think up a set of characteristics which describes them all.

These problems indicate that it is impossible to set down fixed meanings for all words. Humans, it turns out, understand one another not by learning fixed definitions, but by working from a **prototype**, or typical example. A prototypical bird is likely to be something like a robin, with a beak, wings, and stick-like legs, and an ability to fly. A penguin or an emu is still sufficiently like a bird to be regarded as a bird, even though it is not such a 'normal' or prototypical bird. This flexibility allows a great number of things to be classified as birds, even a one-legged, one-winged parrot without a beak.

It is not yet clear how to write this type of flexibility into a linguistic description. We need to pretend things are cut and dried in order to write a useful description of them, on the other hand we have to be aware that they are not. Exactly where the balance should lie is still under discussion.

The meaning of sentences

So far, we have dealt only with the meaning of words. But what about sentences? In fact, the meaning of words tells us quite a lot about the meaning of sentences, since sentences are individual words linked together by means of the syntax. This enables us to understand why a sentence like:

My brother is a spinster

is, if taken literally, contradictory. We would be saying:

My male sibling is an unmarried female

where *male* and *female* are opposites. Some semanticists talk about such sentences as being 'false', in that they could not possibly be 'true': they deal with meaning by working out conditions under which sentences will be either 'true' or 'false'.

The amalgamation of word meaning and syntax does not only enable us to reject anomalous utterances, it also allows us to make deductions about normal sentences. Take the sentence:

The cobra killed a rat.

Our knowledge that *kill* has the properties CAUSE DIE allows us to draw the conclusion that 'The rat died'. In linguistic terminology, *The cobra killed a rat* **entails** 'The rat died'. Similarly, we know that cobras are snakes, so we can conclude that 'A snake caused the rat to die', or going further: 'An animate being, a snake, a cobra, caused an animate being, a mammal, a rat to become not alive'. A large proportion of our ability to understand sentences comes from logical inferences of this type.

After a sentence has been 'unpacked' into its underlying meaning, most linguists assume that semantic representations should be expressed in some type of formal logic.

Formal logical systems can (in theory) provide formulae for the representation of the sentences of any language, and can show the logical relationships which exist between sentences. And logic has the great advantage of being able to show certain ambiguities quite clearly. Take the sentence

All the nice girls love a sailor.

This could either mean: 'Every nice girl loves some sailor or other: Alice loves Joe, Mary loves Bert, and Desdemona loves Billy'. Or it could mean, 'Every nice girl loves one particular sailor: his name is Jack Tar'. Logic provides a precise notation in which the two different structures are clearly shown.

At the moment, it is not clear which type of logic (if any, of those currently in use) is best for language. One promising system is relatively new, devised especially for language by a logician Richard Montague. His approach is known as **Montague semantics**. A number of people working on transformational grammar have tried to use this system to deal with the semantic component of the grammar. But it is not yet clear whether it will become generally accepted, or whether some alternative approach will become more widespread.

Of course, working out logical relationships is not the only way in which humans cope with meaning. In addition, they put their common sense to work. If someone said:

That girl's an elephant.

a strict logical system would reject it as an impossibility, since girls are not elephants. But a human being would try to work out why the speaker said something so apparently idiotic. We will discuss how people do this in the next chapter.

QUESTIONS

1 How might a linguist study the internal relationships between lexical items?
2 What is **inclusion**? Give examples.
3 Distinguish three types of opposites found in language.
4 Why is it impossible to assign firm meanings to some words?
5 What is a **prototype**, and why is this notion important for the study of meaning?
6 How might one represent the meaning of sentences?

PART THREE

The Outer Rings

'When I use a word,' Humpty Dumpty said in a rather scornful tone, 'it means just what I choose it to mean—neither more nor less.'

LEWIS CARROLL

9

Using Language

'This is a self-clearing cafeteria' ran the notice in the student cafeteria. One might expect the plates and cups to put themselves away, judging from other similar phrases in the language, such as *self-cleaning oven*, *self-raising flour*, *self-righting lifeboat*. Yet the majority of students interpreted the phrase as meaning that they, the customers, were expected to clear away their plates. Why? The obvious answer is that they used their common-sense and knowledge of the world to come to the most plausible interpretation in the circumstances, which was not necessarily the one which was most consistent with the linguistic structures.

Pragmatics is the branch of linguistics which studies those aspects of meaning which cannot be captured by semantic theory. In brief, it deals with how speakers use language in ways which cannot be predicted from linguistic knowledge alone. In a narrow sense, it deals with how listeners arrive at the intended meaning of speakers. In its broadest sense, it deals with the general principles followed by human beings when they communicate with one another. It is therefore sometimes light-heartedly referred to as 'the waste-paper-basket of semantics'.

Pragmatics overlaps with **discourse analysis**, which deals with the various devices used by speakers and writers when they knit single sentences together into a coherent and cohesive whole.

These fields are still fairly new, and there is no general agreement yet as to how to deal with them. This chapter outlines a number of recent approaches which have proved helpful.

The cooperative principle

An American philosopher, Paul Grice, is sometimes regarded as the 'father of pragmatics'. Grice emphasized that human beings communicate efficiently because they are by nature helpful to one another. He attempted to specify the principles which underlie this cooperative behaviour, and proposed four 'maxims' or rules of conversation which can jointly be summarized as a general principle: 'Be cooperative'; there are given below.

1 Maxim of Quantity
Give the right amount of information when you talk. If someone at a party asked 'Who's that person with Bob?', a cooperative reply would be 'That's his new girlfriend, Alison'. An uncooperative reply would be an over-brief one, such as 'A girl', or an over-long one, such as 'That's Alison Margaret Jones, born in Kingston, Surrey on 4th July 1970, daughter of Peter and Mary Jones . . . etc.'

2 Maxim of Quality
Be truthful. For example, if someone asked you the name of an unfamiliar animal, such as a platypus, reply truthfully, and don't say 'It's a kookaburra', or 'It's a duck', if you know it's a platypus.

3 Maxim of Relevance
Be relevant. If someone says, 'What's for supper?', give a reply which fits the question, such as 'Fish and chips', and not 'Tables and chairs' or 'Buttercups are yellow'.

4 Maxim of Manner
Be clear and orderly. For example, describe things in the order in which they occurred: 'The plane taxied down the runway, and took off to the west' rather than 'The plane took off to the west and taxied down the runway', which might confuse people as to what actually happened.

At this outline level, the cooperative principle seems like common-sense. It becomes more interesting when we consider how often people apparently break it. In answer to the question: 'What's for supper?' one is likely to receive a reply such as: 'Billy fell down-stairs', which doesn't answer the query. In answer to a question 'Why don't you like Pamela?' one might get the response: 'Pamela's an elephant', which is patently untrue.

Such replies are not evidence against the cooperative principle. On the contrary, they simply show how strongly it works: people are so convinced that the other person in a conversation is being cooperative, that a superficial breakdown in a conversational maxim is treated as important and informative. For example, if someone said: 'What's for supper?' and the reply was the superficially irrelevant one: 'Billy fell downstairs', the hearer is likely to assume that the information about Billy was somehow important, and will fill in the gaps with assumptions such as 'Since Billy was supposed to cook the supper, and he's fallen downstairs, I assume that there isn't any supper ready'. Similarly, if someone told an overt lie, such as 'Pamela's an elephant', the listener would not just think, 'That's impossible', he or she would cast around as to why the speaker had made this comment. In brief, listeners interpret what people say as conforming to the cooperative principle, even when this principle is overtly broken. They draw implications from the utterance which are not strictly there in the linguistic meaning.

The main problem with these Gricean maxims is that they are fairly vague, and the **conversational implicatures** or conclusions which can be drawn are wide and numerous. Some recent work therefore has attempted to specify how humans manage to disentangle what is relevant from the mass of possible inferences they could make.

Speech acts

When a person utters a sequence of words, the speaker is often trying to achieve some effect with those words, an effect which might in some cases have been accomplished by an alternative action. The words 'Get back!' might convey the same notion as a push. A judge's statement: 'I sentence you to five years imprisonment' is not a mere string of words, but has the same effect as if the judge had marched a man along to a prison, and locked him up. In brief, a number of utterances behave somewhat like actions. If this line of reasoning is taken further, one could argue that all utterances are acts of some type. Even an ordinary utterance such as 'Violets are blue' might be regarded as a special type of act, the act of making a statement:

(I state that:) *Violets are blue.*

This overall approach is known as **speech act** theory, and it is another method by which philosophers and linguists have tried to classify the ways in which humans use language, in this case by treating it as parallel to other actions which humans perform.

Proponents of speech act theory try, in the first place, to list the various possible speech acts which a speaker might attempt to perform—statements, requests, queries, commands, promises, placing of bets, and so on. The lists vary from writer to writer, though the overall core tends to be similar. At the heart of the list come statements, questions, and commands:

(I state that:) *It's cold.*
(I ask you:) *What's the time?*
(I command you:) *Go away!*

These are examples of **direct speech acts**: the act is expressed overtly by the most obvious linguistic means. But many speech acts are **indirect**, in that they possess the syntactic structure more usually associated with another act. For example, the following might all be intended as commands, yet only the first has the typical command structure:

Go to bed!
Isn't it past your bedtime?
You should have been in bed long ago.

The first is therefore a direct speech act, but the second two are indirect speech acts.

But how do people know which speech act is intended, if each act can use the syntactic structure typically associated with one of the others? A possible answer is to specify **happiness conditions** or **felicity conditions**—circumstances under which it would be appropriate to interpret something as a particular type of speech act. For example, if a genuine command has been given, the hearer must be physically capable of carrying it out, and must be able to identify the object(s) involved. Even this partial statement of the felicity conditions for commands would probably enable someone to identify 'Pick up that book!' and 'That book oughtn't to be on the floor' as genuine commands, and 'Go jump in the lake!' and 'Gird up thy loins!' as pseudo-commands.

If we could fully identify the felicity conditions for each type of speech act, then we would have moved some way towards understanding how humans use language—though obviously, the various direct and indirect speech acts used depend on the social situation. In British English, speech acts become less direct as one moves up the politeness scale. A polite command is rarely expressed directly.

Of the three below, the first, a direct command, would be made perhaps only to a young child:

Shut the door!
I wonder if you'd mind shutting the door?
There's quite a draught in here.

This can confuse foreigners quite considerably: 'Why did that man look offended when I said, "Pass the salt"?' asked one puzzled visitor. This type of study therefore overlaps with sociolinguistics.

Remembered frameworks

The field of artificial intelligence (AI) has provided a further approach to how people understand one another. AI makes proposals about how to simulate intelligent systems on computers. The original problem was one of finding out how computers could be made to cope with inexplicit and superficially irrelevant conversations:

Salesman: *Pink sinks are the latest fashion, madam.*
Customer: *My dish-washer's red.*

A solution proposed for the computer might also be one utilized by humans. Knowledge, it was suggested, might be stored in the form of stereotypical situations, or **frames**. These memorized frameworks are adapted to fit in with present reality, so they are altered as required. So, for example, a person might have a frame representing a typical kitchen, and would have 'slots' in the frame for a sink, a cooker, a dish-washer and so on. A superficially disjointed conversation, such as the one above, would become quite coherent when considered in relation to the 'kitchen frame' in a person's mind. Furthermore, the speakers in this conversation clearly have a certain amount of mutual knowledge, in that they both have a similar outline kitchen frame. Another way of dealing with human interaction, therefore, is to specify both the relevant frames and the mutual knowledge held in common by the participants.

Discourse analysis

So far, we have concentrated on cases in which people made sense of quite strange disjointed utterances. However, when we use language, we do not necessarily do so in a random and unstructured way. Both conversation and written texts have various devices for welding together miscellaneous utterances into a cohesive whole.

Compare the two accounts of George's meal below:

A   George ate the curry with delight. Curry had always been George's favourite food. The curry was subtly flavoured. George detected hints of cumin and coriander in the curry. Cumin and coriander are George's favourite spices.

B   George ate the curry with delight. This type of food had always been his favourite. The dish was subtly flavoured, and in it he detected hints of his favourite spices, cumin and coriander.

The two versions are more or less the same as far as semantic content is concerned, and the syntax is fairly similar. Nevertheless, there is a lot of difference between the two. The second is both stylistically better, and more normal-sounding. The first appears to have been written sentence by sentence, without any attention to the overall effect. In the second, various devices have been used in order to link the sentences together into a cohesive whole: after its first occurrence, the word *curry* has been replaced by alternative words *this type of food*, *the dish*, and by the pronoun *it*. Similarly, *George* has been replaced by *he*, and in some places, the order of words has been altered so as to maintain the smooth connections, as when *in it* was brought to the front of its clause. In addition, some of the original sentences have been joined together.

Discourse analysis is the study which deals with this topic. It overlaps with **stylistics**, the study of linguistics and literature. Devices which maintain the smooth flow of communication are particularly important in written language, where there is no one available to clarify unclear points. However, many of these devices are also used in ordinary conversation. Consider two versions of the same dialogue:

A   Edna: *Someone ought to lock up Fred.*
Minnie: *Fred is a disgrace.*
Edna: *Someone caught Fred peeping at the new lodger through the bathroom window.*
Minnie: *What is the name of the new lodger? Is the name of the new lodger Arabella or Annabel?*

B   Edna: *Fred ought to be locked up.*
Minnie: *That man's a disgrace.*
Edna: *He was caught peeping through the bathroom window at the new lodger.*

Minnie: *What's her name? Is it Arabella or Annabel?*

The first version sounds stilted and odd, even though by itself, each sentence is well-formed. The second version sounds far more like an ordinary conversation. It contains devices similar to those used in the piece of prose about George and his curry: after the first occurrence of *Fred*, the alternative phrase *that man* and the pronoun *he* was used. The third sentence has been changed into the passive, in order to keep Fred at the centre of attention. And so on. The overall result is that the whole dialogue becomes linked together into a cohesive whole, something that people who know a language do automatically—though people learning a second language usually have to be taught this skill, as the devices used vary in their details from language to language.

Taking it in turns

Conversation is not just a case of linking sentences together. On a more basic level, it fits into a conventional framework. Consider the 'dialogue' below:

Mother: *And how's my pretty little darling then?*
Baby: *Ugh . . . Ugh.*
Mother: *O what a nice bit of wind that was! You must be feeling better!*
Baby: *Goo, goo.*

This brief snatch of 'conversation' illustrates one important fact about human speech: people take it in turns to talk. Even if one of the participants cannot speak, the other one pretends that the non-talker has taken their turn. But we can go further than simply noting the phenomenon of turn-taking. We can, in addition, describe how a typical conversation might proceed. The speakers are taking part in a social ritual partially prescribed by convention. In a dialogue, utterances very often occur in pairs, which are sometimes known as **exchanges** or **adjacency pairs**:

Question: *What's the time?*
Answer: *Ten past three.*

Greeting: *Hi, Jo.*
Greeting: *Why hallo Bill.*

Offer: *Would you like a cup of coffee?*
Acceptance: *Yes, please.*

Apology: *I'm terribly sorry.*
Minimization: *Please don't mention it.*

Paired utterances are not, of course, inevitable, and triple utterances are also frequent:

Question: *What's the time?*
Answer: *Ten past three.*
Acknowledgement: *Thanks.*

Conversations, then, typically follow a predictable format, exchanges are selected from a number of commonly used types. The options chosen by a particular speaker on a particular occasion depend on the social situation, so this type of study has in recent years become a part of sociolinguistics, the topic of the next chapter.

QUESTIONS

1 What is **pragmatics**?
2 What four conversational maxims form the **cooperative principle**?
3 What is **speech act** theory?
4 What are **frames**?
5 Explain two ways in which a person might make a piece of prose more cohesive.
6 Explain what is meant by **adjacency pairs**. Give two examples.

10

Language and Society

Sociolinguistics is often defined as the study of language and society. Whereas many linguists concentrate on discovering unity beneath the diversity of human languages, sociolinguists try to analyse the social factors which lead to this diversity. In brief, sociolinguists are interested in language differences, and especially in variation within a particular language.

The notion of a language

Perhaps the first question that a sociolinguist needs to ask is, 'What is a language?' Can the notion of 'a language' be defined geographically? Can it be equated with nationality? Or should a language be defined by the mutual intelligibility of its speakers?

The answer to all these questions appears to be 'no'. A geographical definition of a language would separate Australian, British and American English, which is obviously unsatisfactory. Nationality is a vague notion which has little to do with the language a man speaks. Numerous Soviet Jews, for example, regard themselves as essentially Jewish, yet speak Russian. Mutual intelligibility is of little help, since a Glaswegian and a Cockney are likely to find it harder to understand one another than a Dutchman and German who are considered to be speaking distinct languages. And there is no objective linguistic criterion which can be applied. Dutch and German are not only mutually intelligible, they are also structurally more alike than some of the so-called dialects of Chinese.

Faced with this dilemma, sociolinguists prefer to start with the notion of a **speech community** rather than a 'language'. And they define a speech community as any group of people who consider that they speak the same language. Consequently, Dutch and

German must be regarded as separate languages, since, in spite of their similarities, the Dutch consider that they speak Dutch and the Germans consider that they speak German. And all the Chinese dialects must be classified as one language, because, in spite of far-reaching differences, their speakers all consider they speak Chinese.

Dialect and accent

Within a speech community, there is considerable language variation. The speech of its members varies according to many factors, including geographical location, age, occupation, socio-economic status, ethnic group and sex.

The most obvious type of variety in a speech community is the use of different **dialects**. A dialect is usually associated with a particular geographical area, such as the Geordie and Cockney dialects of English, which are spoken in Tyneside and London respectively. The term 'dialect' refers to a far greater difference than mere pronunciation. The Lancashire dialect differs from standard British English in sound system, syntax and vocabulary, with phrases such as, *I don't want for to go*, *summat* for 'something', *nowt* for 'nothing'. American English ranks as a different dialect from British English, with phonological innovations such as nasal vowels, and constructions such as 'I kinda figured maybe' and 'He said for you not to worry'.

Unfortunately, in everyday usage, the term dialect is often confused with the word **accent**. An accent refers only to a difference in pronunciation. A Scotsman and a Londoner are likely to speak English with different accents. But if the underlying system and the vocabulary are the same, they will be speaking the same dialect. In fact, although a considerable number of local accents are still found in Britain, dialects are dying out, due to the influence of education, radio and television.

Specialized styles (registers)

More interesting to sociolinguists is variation within a single geographical area. This is of two main types: variation within the speech of a single person, and variation between people. These two interact, and it is not always possible to separate them. However, let us begin by considering the variation which exists in the speech of any one person.

Every native speaker of a language is normally in command of several different styles of speech (sometimes called **registers**) which are varied according to the needs of the situation. For example, the same person might utter any of the following three sentences, depending on the circumstances:

1 '*I should be grateful if you would make less noise.*'
2 '*Please be quiet.*'
3 '*Shut up.*'

Here the utterances range from a 'high' or formal style, down to a 'low' or informal one. Note that the use of an inappropriate register is one source of humour in English, as in:

> *Scintillate, scintillate, globule lucific,*
> *Fain would I fathom thy nature specific.*

This seems amusing because of the use of a formal style to 'translate' a rhyme associated with an informal nursery setting:

> *Twinkle, twinkle, little star*
> *How I wonder what you are.*

The formality–informality scale overlaps with another variable, namely the subject-matter of the conversation. Many activities and occupations have a specialized vocabulary and (in a few cases) specialized syntax. If you are playing a ball game, you need to know that 'zero' is *a duck* in cricket, *love* in tennis, and *nil* in soccer. The language of headlines or advertizing, on the other hand, has a fairly normal vocabulary, but a specialized syntax. In both cases, verbs are often omitted: 'Giant waves down *Queen Mary*'s funnel' (news-paper headline). 'Musk. The missing link between animal and man. Earthy. Primitive. Fiercely masculine' (cosmetic advertisement).

In England, the use of an inappropriate style is not considered a serious social blunder in most instances. In any case, there is often a considerable amount of overlap between the use of the different styles. It would not matter whether you said 'Hallo' or 'Good morning' to your neighbour. In some other cultures, however, the social situation requires a far greater degree of rigidity. An extreme example is found in Java, where society is divided into three distinct social groups. At the top are the aristocrats. In the middle are the townsfolk, and at the bottom are the farmers. Each of these groups has a distinct style of speech associated with it. The top level of speech is used primarily between aristocrats who do not know one another very well, but also by a townsman if he happens to be addressing a high government official. The middle level of speech is used between townsmen who are not close friends, and by peasants when addressing their social superiors. The lowest level is used between peasants, or by an aristocrat or townsman when talking to a peasant, and between close friends on any level. Furthermore, it is the form of language used by parents to their children, so it is the style learned first by all Javanese children. However, as they grow up, children are expected to shift to addressing their parents in a more formal style, even though their parents continue to speak to them in the lowest style!

Another example of a situation where it is essential to speak in the appropriate style is found among the Subanun, a Philippine tribe. If you want a drink, it is not sufficient simply to give the Subanun equivalent of English, 'Please may I have a drink'. This utterance might cause a Subanun speaker to praise you for your fluent Subanun, but he would not get you a drink! Drinking, particularly the drinking of beer, is a highly ritualized activity which progresses through a number of stages. At each stage, there is an appropriate style of speech, and your advancement in Subanun society depends on how well you can cope with this.

Change in language styles

The linguistic situation found in Java, and that surrounding the Subanun ritual drinking, reflects the social situation. This is not necessarily static. Any change in the social relationships is likely to be mirrored in changing language styles. An example of a change of this type occurred in the gradual meaning change in the two forms of the pronoun *you* in European languages.

Originally, in Latin, there was a singular form *tu* and a plural form *vos*. For some reason (the cause is disputed), the plural came to be used as a polite form of address for speaking to a single person in authority. One theory is that when there were two Roman emperors —one in the east at Constantinople, the other in the west in Rome—it became customary to address each of them as *vos*, since both emperors were implicitly being addressed at the same time. This began a general trend for using *vos* to anyone in authority. It gradually became customary for a working-class person to address a member of the aristocracy as *vos*, while the upper classes still used *tu* to a lower-class individual. Meanwhile, as a mark of respect, the aristocracy began to address one another as *vos*, although the lower classes continued to address one another as *tu*. This situation is

	To upper class	*To lower class*
Upper class	vos	tu
Lower class	vos	tu

Fig. 47

shown in Figure 47. This linguistic situation reflected the social situation. There existed a feudal society in which the power of one class over another was all-important.

However, as feudalism died out, so did this structuring of *tu* and *vos*. Gradually (according to one theory), people ceased to feel such respect for those in power, and instead, they merely felt remote from them. *Vos* (it is claimed) came to be not so much a mark of respect, as one of non-intimacy. *Tu* came to be thought of as indicating intimacy, companionship and solidarity. People involved in friendships or close relationships started to call one another *tu* irrespective of the power situation. And this is the state of affairs today in the numerous European languages which have two forms of the word *you*.

The 'power' to 'solidarity' switch is possibly only one of several factors involved in the change from *vos* to *tu*, and some have disputed its importance. However, a similar phenomenon seems to be occurring in other parts of the world also: in India, in the Hindi and Gujerati languages, there was formerly a power pattern shown in the non-reciprocal nature of the forms of address between husband and wife, and older and younger brother. Nowadays this is dying out. Reciprocal relations are gradually becoming more important than the power of one person over another, and members of Indian families are beginning to address one another with the intimate *you* forms.

Charting phonological variation

So far, in our discussion of language styles, we have talked only about vocabulary and syntax. However, phonological variation, both between speakers and within a single speaker, is immensely important as a reflection of various social factors. Speakers of a language alter their phonology to suit a particular situation, often without realizing it. For example, someone from Devon is likely to pronounce the [r] in a word such as *farm* when chatting with friends at home, but would probably attempt to suppress it in a formal interview in London. In this case, the speaker may well be aware of the change in pronunciation. On the other hand, few speakers of standard British English realize that in informal situations they often omit the [t] at the end of words such as *last* in phrases such as *last thing*.

At one time, it was thought that such variation was fairly random, and that no precise statements could be made about it. But an American sociolinguist, William Labov, showed that this was not so. In a piece of work which has now become famous he examined the pronunciation of words such as *car*, *park* in New York. New Yorkers sometimes pronounce an [r] in these words, and sometimes do not. Although Labov was unable to tell which words were likely to be pronounced with [r], and which without, he found that he could predict the percentage of [r] sounds which each socio-economic class and each age group would use in any given type of speech.

Labov started his work on [r] in a highly amusing way. First, he found out which departments were on the fourth floor in three New York department stores. He then asked as many shop assistants as possible a question such as 'Excuse me, where are children's coats?' The answer to each of these queries was, of course, 'On the *fourth floor*', which included two words that could each contain an [r]. It is well-known that sales-staff tend to mimic the speech of their customers, and, as Labov predicted, he found that in the store that was considered socially inferior, the number of [r] sounds was low, under 20%. In the middle-ranking store, [r] was inserted about 50% of the time, and in the store considered socially superior, [r] was used over 60% of the time. These preliminary results clearly showed that the use of [r] in New York was a useful guide to social status.

After this preliminary survey, Labov then examined the speech of each class of person in more detail. Perhaps predictably, he found that [r] was inserted much more frequently in careful speech and in the reading of word lists than in casual speech. This was true of all social classes. There was, however, one unexpected finding. When reading word lists, lower-middle-class speakers inserted [r] more often than upper-middle-class speakers—even though in casual speech, the situation was reversed, with lower-middle-class speech containing fewer [r] sounds. This suggests that lower-middle-class speakers are more consciously aware of speech as an indicator of social class, and are making efforts to improve their status.

Phonological variation in British English

At first, one might assume Labov's results to be unique, in that they possibly reflected an American social situation that was unlikely to be paralleled elsewhere. But in England, a similar state of affairs has been found in the speech of people living in Norwich. Consider the differing pronunciations of words ending in *-ing*. Sometimes, Norwich inhabitants pronounce the *-ing* as in standard English, and at other times they say *walkin'*, *talkin'*, *singin'*, with [n] instead of [ŋ]. When the distribution of *-ing* was examined more closely, a number of interesting facts emerged. First of all, and predictably, the proportion of *-ing* forms was much higher in careful speech than in casual speech for all social classes. For example, those classified as lower-working-class used *-ing* around 70% of the time when they were asked to read word lists, but hardly ever in casual speech. On the other hand, middle-middle-class speakers used *-ing* 100% of the time in word lists, but only around 70% of the time in casual speech.

Second (and perhaps surprisingly), upper-working-class Norwich inhabitants were found to behave in a very similar way to lower-middle-class New Yorkers. For this social group, there was an enormous discrepancy between the type of speech used in word lists (*-ing* occurred 95% of the time), and that used in casual speech (*-ing* occurred only 13% of the time). Once again, speakers with a relatively low social status appeared to be attempting to 'better themselves' by speaking in a style they regarded as superior to their normal speech. The Norwich situation is illustrated in Figure 48.

A further analysis of the use of *-ing* by upper-working-class speakers revealed an unexpected sex difference. Women were found to use *-ing* more often than men. This suggests that 'changes from above' (Labov's term for changes of which speakers are consciously aware) may well be initiated mainly by women. There is further evidence that other changes are taking place 'from below', that is, below the level of conscious awareness. These changes appeared to be initiated by working-class men. For example, in Norwich, the vowel sound in words such as *night*, *rye*, *side*, is moving towards the sound *oy* [ɔɪ]. This change is furthest advanced in the speech of working-class men. It has been suggested that perhaps unconsciously, people admire working-class men and associate them with strength and virility, and, without realizing it, adopt features found in their speech. This pattern seems not to be unique to Norwich, but a general phenomenon found in other areas of the world also.

Fig. 48

These examples of phonological variation are highly informative. They provide an objective reflection of various social factors such as socio-economic class, ethnic group, age and sex. The effect of any one of these factors on language can be analysed, and so can the interaction between them. For example, in one study of the interaction between ethnic group and age in Boston, a particular pronunciation of [o] was found to be associated with elderly Jews, and with Italians of all ages. The younger members of the Jewish community, who were mostly highly educated, had abandoned it, perhaps because they regarded it as non-standard. The Italians, on the other hand, tended to favour it as a mark of Italian identity. Such studies can shed interesting light on the pressures and attitudes within particular communities.

Social networks

Labov-type surveys rely on collecting data from a random sample of individuals. Their speech is analysed for various key characteristics, which are then correlated with their social background. The result, perhaps not surprisingly, suggests that human society is somewhat like a layer-cake, with different socio-economic layers stacked up on top of one another. In one respect, this is a useful insight into the way societies function. But, as with many surveys, the result is oversimplified. In practice, people do not normally live in such clear-cut layers: someone from the so-called working class might well have middle class friends and neighbours.

In fact, human beings tend to cluster into **social networks**, groups of people who regularly interact with one another. A detailed study of the social networks within one particular speech community can provide a useful corrective to Labov-type studies, which tend to suggest humans are rigidly stratified. Network studies can provide a more realistic picture of the way people interact in real life. Furthermore, if a sociolinguist manages to be introduced into a network, its members are more likely to chat in a natural way than in a Labov-type survey in which it is sometimes difficult to observe people speaking 'normally'.

The British linguist Leslie Milroy pioneered the linguistic study of social networks with a study of three communities in Belfast. She was introduced into each group as 'a friend of a friend'. This ensured that she was accepted, and that people would talk relatively normally in front of her: when one youth tried to show off by talking in a somewhat affected way, his friend punched him and shouted: 'Come on, you're not on television now, you know'.

Networks can be of high density, when the same people tend to work, play, and live together. On the other hand, they can be of low density, when people only have a small amount of contact with any one network, in that they may live in one area, work in another, and travel elsewhere for their social life (Figure 49).

When Milroy examined her data, she discovered a number of things which would not have been detectable in a Labov-type

High density network   Low density network

Fig. 49

survey. For example, Labov's work suggested that men and women's speech tended to differ, with women on the whole being closer to the prestige norm. Milroy found this pattern also in Belfast overall, but with some interesting subtleties. When she examined the three communities separately, and charted the occurrence of the way [a] was pronounced by people of different age and both sexes, she found some modification of the overall pattern. In the oldest, most tightly-knit, and most traditional community, she found that the predicted pattern of male-female difference was most prominent. But in the other two, which were newer, and fairly loose-knit, this pattern was less evident, and was even reversed among the younger women of one community. This suggests that a blurring of sex differentiation in language may be linked with the break-up of close-knit networks. Findings such as this indicate that linguistic variation needs to be considered from at least two angles: from the point of view of a broad Labov-type survey based on a random sample of people, but also from a close-up view of a number of social networks.

Language and sex

Possible sex differences in language usage have recently attracted a lot of attention.

First, we need to sort out whether women really do speak differently from men. People's impressions are not necessarily correct: it is often assumed, for example, that women talk more than men, whereas almost all research on the topic has demonstrated the opposite, that men talk more than women. Similarly, it is sometimes claimed that women use 'empty' adjectives, such as *divine*, *charming*, *cute*, yet this type of description is possibly more usually used by (presumably male) writers in popular newspapers to describe women.

Furthermore, some characteristics which have been attributed to women turn out to be far more widespread. For example, women have been claimed to use tentative phrases such as 'kind of', 'sort of' in place of straight statements: 'Bill is kind of short', instead of 'Bill is short'. They have also been accused of using question intonation in response to queries: 'About eight o'clock?' as a reply to: 'What time's dinner?' Yet this insecure style of conversation seems to be typical of 'powerless' people, those who are somewhat nervous and afraid of antagonizing others. Powerless people come from either sex.

The most consistent difference found between men and women within the western world is a tendency for women to speak in a way that is closer to the prestige standard. In colloquial terms, they speak 'better' than men. No one is quite sure why this is so, and several explanations have been proposed, which may all be partially right. For example, women may be pressurized by society to behave in a 'ladylike' manner, and 'speaking nicely' may be part of this. Or because they are the main child-rearers, they may subconsciously speak in a way which will enable their children to progress socially. Or they may tend to have jobs which rely on communication, rather than on strength. All these factors, and others, appear to be relevant.

In recent years, particularly among employed women, the differences between men's and women's speech appears to be diminishing. Such studies, then, provide further evidence of the importance of language in reflecting social attitudes and social changes.

Multilingual communities

The types of variation discussed so far all occur within a single language. But sociolinguists are also interested in variation between languages, particularly in bilingual or multilingual communities. Sociolinguistically, this is not necessarily very different from variation within a single language. In some cultures, a changed social situation is marked not by a change in style, but by a change in the actual language spoken, as in the light-hearted saying attributed to the Holy Roman Emperor Charles V, 'I speak Spanish to God, Italian to women, French to men, and German to my horse.'

For example, in Sauris, a small community of north-eastern Italy, high in the Carnian Alps, a quite remarkable linguistic situation exists. The inhabitants use three different languages in the course of their everyday life: a German dialect, Italian and Friulian (a Romance dialect). Italian is the language of organized religion, and also that used in schools. Friulian is the language used by men in the local bars. And German is the language used in the home. It is highly unusual to hear German outside the home, though it was observed on one occasion when a furious woman burst into a bar and upbraided her husband for not having returned home at the time he was expected!

A study of the ways in which these multiple languages are used is particularly important for **language planning**, a situation in which a government or education authority attempts to manipulate the linguistic situation in a particular direction. This is more likely to be successful if existing uses of a language are gradually extended, since the sudden imposition of a particular language by decree may well result in failure.

However, multilingual societies in which all the speakers are proficient in all the languages spoken are something of a rarity. Quite often, one language, or simplified language, is adopted as a common means of communication. This can happen either naturally, or as a result of language planning. A common language of this type is sometimes known as a **lingua franca**. A couple of millennia ago, Latin spread around the Mediterranean countries in this way. In India today, English tends to be a lingua franca: Hindi speakers from the north are likely to communicate in English with people from the south who mostly speak one of the Dravidian languages. The artificial language, Esperanto, is sometimes proposed as a candidate for a world lingua franca.

Pidgins and creoles

Adopting a lingua franca is not the only solution to the problem of communication between groups of people speaking different languages. In some cases, a **pidgin** develops.

A **pidgin** is a restricted language system which arises in order to fulfil essential communication needs among people with no common language. It is no one's first language, and is used at first in a limited set of circumstances. Such a system typically develops on trade routes and in coastal areas.

A pidgin is usually based on one language, though it soon acquires an admixture of other languages, as well as independent constructions of its own. For example, Tok Pisin (also known as Melanesian Pidgin English and Neo-Melanesian) which is spoken in Papua New Guinea, is based on English, and many of the words sound somewhat like English ones:

Mi go long taun. 'I go/went to the town'.
Yu wokabaut long rot. 'You walk/walked along the road'.

But there are plenty of others, which cannot be predicted from English, such as *lotu* 'church', *diwai* 'tree', *susu* 'milk'. In addition, it has acquired syntactic constructions which do not figure in English. For example, there is a consistent distinction between verbs with an object ('transitive' verbs) which take the ending *-im*, as with *bagarapim* 'wreck', and those without ('intransitive' verbs) as in *bagarap* 'collapse', 'break down':

Mi bagarapim ka bilong yu. 'I crashed your car'.
Ka bilong mi i bagarap. 'My car broke down'.

Another innovation is the particle *i* which usually has to be placed before the verb (as in the second sentence above).

The phonology, syntax, and lexicon are simpler in a pidgin than in an ordinary language. There are fewer phonemes. In Tok Pisin, [p] and [f] are often merged, so are [s] and [ʃ], and there are only five vowels. English 'fish' was borrowed as *pis*, and English 'ship' as *sip*. In order to avoid confusion, 'piss' (urinate) became *pispis*, and 'sheep' becomes *sipsip*. There are very few word endings, the sentences have a simple structure, and there is a small vocabulary. One or two items stretch over a wide area, as with the following uses of the word *pikinini* 'child':

pikinini man 'son' (lit. child man).
pikinini meri 'daughter' (lit. child woman).
pikinini hos 'foal' (lit. child horse).
pikinini pis 'minnow' (lit. child fish).
pikinini bilong rais 'rice kernels' (lit. child of rice).
pikinini bilong diwai 'fruit of tree' (lit. child of tree).

Sometimes, pidgins die out of their own accord. At other times they increase in importance, and become used in more and more areas of life. If someone then acquires a pidgin as a first language —perhaps because of intermarriage between people whose only common language is the pidgin—the language has then become a **creole**.

Once it has become a creole, the system tends to develop rapidly. Speech is speeded up, the syntax becomes more complex, and extra vocabulary items are created. Fairly soon, if it continues to develop, a creole is likely to be indistinguishable from a 'full' language.

In some circumstances, however, a creole can be devoured by its parent. If a creole is spoken in an area where the base language is also used, then there may be social pressure on the creole speakers to speak the base, which often has more prestige. Therefore, little by little, the creole becomes **decreolized**, as words and constructions from the base language replace the creole ones.

The study of pidgins and creoles has grown rapidly, because their implications and interest spread far beyond sociolinguistics. They are valuable for the insights they provide into language change, and some people have claimed that they shed light on language universals—that they present language in a stripped down and basic state. This claim is controversial, but the interest it has aroused has increased the attention given to the topic. Only time will tell whether such grandiose claims are justified.

QUESTIONS

1   What problems arise in an attempt to define the notion of 'a language'?
2   Distinguish between **dialect** and **accent**.
3   Give an example of a change in social situation which is reflected in a changed linguistic situation.
4   Which socio-economic class is likely to show the greatest phonological variation within its speech, and why?
5   What is **language planning**, and how might it be carried out effectively?
6   What is a **pidgin**, and how may it be distinguished from a **creole**?

11

Language and Mind

Psycholinguistics is often defined as the study of language and the mind. It explores what goes on in the human mind as an individual acquires, comprehends, produces and stores language. Such a study covers an enormous range of topics, and no two psycholinguists agree on exactly the ground which it covers. One reason for this disagreement is that psycholinguistics overlaps with a somewhat wider study, sometimes called the **psychology of communication**, which looks at language alongside other human methods of communication, such as the use of gesture and facial expressions.

This chapter outlines some of the work going on in three 'core' psycholinguistic topics:

How humans acquire language.
How humans comprehend speech.
How humans produce speech.

Psycholinguistic evidence

Since the mind cannot be directly observed, psycholinguists have to devise ways of finding out how it works. They get their evidence from two main sources: observation of spontaneous utterances, on the one hand, and psycholinguistic experiments, on the other.

Spontaneous utterances which deviate from the norm in some way are the most informative. We can learn considerably more from a child's mistake such as *foots* instead of 'feet', or someone who said *geranium* instead of 'hydrangea', than we can from a perfect flow of speech.

However, ordinary speech is somewhat messy, in that there are dozens of different factors which have to be taken into account when utterances are analysed. Psycholinguists therefore devise experiments in which the number of variable factors can be controlled, and the results can be accurately measured. They might, for example, set subjects a 'lexical decision task', in which they time how long it takes a person to recognize a word as being a word, or reject a nonsense sequence such as *vleesidence* as a non-word.

But this type of methodology presents a problem, sometimes called the 'experimental paradox'. The more carefully an experiment is devised so as to limit variables, the more subjects are put into an unnatural situation, in which they are likely to behave oddly. On the other hand, the more one allows a situation to be like 'real life', the less one is able to sort out the various interacting factors.

Ideally, major topics should be tackled both by observing spontaneous speech and by devising experiments. And when the results coincide, this is a sign that progress is being made.

Acquiring language

The so-called 'innateness question' has been a burning issue over the last quarter century. Exactly how much language is pre-programmed within the human mind? Do humans have a genetically imprinted 'Universal Grammar', as Chomsky suggests? Or were the rudiments of language invented by a clever cave-man and handed down from generation to generation? No detailed solution has yet been found to these questions. But by examining them, we are slowly acquiring a greater understanding of the nature of human language.

One point in particular has become clearer: language has all the hallmarks of **maturationally controlled behaviour**. It used to be thought that animal behaviour could be divided into two types: that which was inborn and natural (for example, dogs naturally bark), and that which was learned and unnatural (dogs may be taught to beg). It turns out, however, that this division is by no means clear-cut and may be misleading. Many types of behaviour develop 'naturally' at a certain age, provided that the surrounding environment is adequate. Such behaviour is maturationally controlled, and sexual activity is a typical example. Arguments as to whether it is inborn or learnt are futile. Both nature and nurture are important. Innate potentialities lay down the framework, and within this framework, there is wide variation depending on the environment.

When individuals reach a crucial point in their maturation, they are biologically in a state of readiness for learning the behaviour. They would not learn it at this time without a biological trigger, and conversely, the biological trigger could not be activated if there was nobody around from whom they could learn the behaviour.

From the age of around eighteen months human infants are in a state of language readiness. The urge for language to emerge at this time is very strong, and only very extraordinary circumstances will suppress it—as in the case of Genie, a Californian teenager who from the age of twenty months had been confined to one small room, and had been physically punished by her father if she made any sounds. Naturally, she was without speech when she was found. But all normal children, and some abnormal ones, will begin to speak if they hear language going on around them.

The content-process controversy

The realization that language is maturationally controlled means that most psycholinguists now agree that human beings are innately programmed to speak. But they cannot agree on exactly *what* is innate. In particular, they cannot decide to what extent (if any) language ability is separate from other cognitive abilities.

All researchers agree that there is extraordinary similarity in the speech development of English children. Children who could not possibly be acquainted go through similar stages in their development, and also make similar mistakes. The implications of this coincidence are hotly disputed. On the one hand, there are those who consider that this uniformity of speech development indicates that children innately *contain* a blueprint for language: this view represents a so-called **content** approach. Extreme supporters of this view suggests that children may have a universal framework imprinted on their brains.

On the other hand, there are those who support a **process** approach, and argue that children could not possibly contain specific language universals. Instead, they are innately geared to *processing* linguistic data, for which they utilize a puzzle-solving ability which is closely related to other cognitive skills.

A further group of people point to the social nature of language, and the role of parents. Children, they argue, are social beings who have a great need to interact with those around them. Furthermore, all over the world, child-carers tend to talk about the same sort of things, chatting mainly about food, clothes and other objects in the immediate environment. **Motherese** or **caregiver language** has fairly similar characteristics everywhere: the caregivers slow down their rate of speech, and speak in slow, well-formed utterances, with quite a lot of repetition. People who stress these social aspects of language claim that there is no need to search for complex innate mechanisms: social interaction with caring caregivers is sufficient to cause language to develop.

This latter view is turning out to be something of an exaggeration. The fact that parents make it easier for children to learn language does not explain why they are so quick to acquire it: intelligent chimps exposed to intensive sign language rarely get beyond 200 words and two-word sequences. Furthermore, language seems to be due to something more than a desire to communicate. There is at least one strange child on record who acquired fluent language, but did not use it to communicate. He spoke only monologues to himself, and refused to interact with others.

The whole controversy is far from being solved, though psycholinguists hope that the increasing amount of work being done on the acquisition of languages other than English may shed more light on the topic. It is possible, however, that we shall never unravel the mystery entirely: it seems likely that children use an inbuilt linguistic ability to solve general intelligence problems, and also their natural puzzle-solving abilities to solve linguistic problems. With this kind of intertwining, the various strands may be inextricably interwoven.

The rule-governed nature of child language

In spite of the numerous controversies surrounding child language, psycholinguists are at least in agreement on one major point. Children are not simply imitating what they hear going on around them as if they were parrots. The learning processes involved are far more complex. From the moment they begin to talk, children seem to be aware that language is **rule-governed**, and they are engaged in an active search for the rules which underlie the language to which they are exposed. Child language is never at any time a haphazard conglomeration of random words, or a sub-standard version of adult speech. Instead, every child at every stage possesses a grammar with rules of its own even though the system will be simpler than that of an adult. For example, when children first use negatives, they normally use a simple rule: 'Put *no* or *not* in front of the sentence.' This results in consistent negative sentences which the child could not possibly have heard from an adult:

No play that.
No Fraser drink all tea.

This rule is generally superseded by another which says: 'Insert the negative after the first NP.' This also produces a consistent set of sentences which the child is unlikely to have heard from an adult:

He no bite you.
That no mummy.

A rather more obvious example of the rule-governed nature of child language are forms such as *mans*, *foots*, *gooses*, which children produce frequently. Such plurals occur even when a child understands and responds correctly to the adult forms *men*, *feet*, *geese*. This is clear proof that children's own rules of grammar are more important to them than mere imitation.

Children do not, however, formulate a new rule overnight, and suddenly replace the old one with this new one. Instead, there is considerable fluctuation between the old and the new. The new construction appears at first in a limited number of places. A child might first use the word *what* in a phrase with a single verb,

What mummy doing?
What daddy doing?
What Billy doing?

then only gradually extend it to other verbs, as in

What kitty eating?
What mummy sewing?

This process is somewhat like the way in which an alteration creeps from word to word in language change (Chapter 12).

Attention to the ways in which children move from one rule to another has shown that language acquisition is not as uniform as was once thought. Different children use different strategies for acquiring speech. For example, some seem to concentrate on the overall rhythm, and slot in words with the same general sound pattern, whereas others prefer to deal with more abstract slots. Of particular interest is work which looks at how children cope with different languages. This enables researchers to see if children have any universal expectations about how language behaves, or whether they wait and see what their own particular language offers.

Learning the meaning of words

Children have to learn not only the syntax and sounds of their language, but also the meaning of words. This turns out to be more complicated than some people suppose. For a start, it probably takes some time for children to discover that words can refer to separate things. At first, they probably think that a word such as *milk* refers to a whole generalized ritual, something uttered as a mug is placed in front of them. Later they, discover that words have meanings which can be applied to individual objects and actions.

People often remark on children's overgeneralizations. Youngsters may call any type of small thing a *crumb*: a crumb, a small beetle, or a speck of dirt, or they may apply the word *moon* to any kind of light. An idea popular in the last century was that children see the world through a mental fog. They are able only to grasp broad outlines, which they then narrow down. But this turns out to be an oversimplification, because children's overgeneralizations are often quite specific, and quite odd. One child referred to a shiny green leaf as a moon! A possible explanation is that she was working from a prototype (Chapter 8) which was unlike the adult's prototype. This child had apparently taken a picture of a shiny yellow crescent moon as a prototypical moon, and re-applied the word *moon* to anything which had the approximate shape of the original, as well as one of its other characteristics. The leaf was vaguely crescent shaped, and also shiny. This interesting idea is currently being explored by researchers.

Recognizing words

Understanding speech is not the simple matter it appears to be at first sight. Most people assume that comprehension involves being a passive recipient of someone else's message. Hearers, it is often supposed, behave like secretaries taking down a mental dictation. They mentally record the message, then read it back to themselves.

This assumption turns out to be quite wrong. For a start, it is physically impossible to recognize each separate sound, speech is just too fast. Understanding language is an *active*, not a passive process. Hearers jump to conclusions on the basis of partial information. This has been demonstrated in various experiments. For example, listeners were asked to interpret the following sentences, in which the first sound of the final word was indistinct:

Paint the fence and the ?ate.
Check the calandar and the ?ate.
Here's the fishing gear and the ?ate.

The subjects claimed to hear *gate* in the first sentence, *date* in the second, and *bait* in the third.

Since recognizing words involves quite a lot of guesswork, how do speakers make the guesses? Suppose someone had heard 'She saw a do—'. Would the hearer check through the possible candidates one after the other, *dog*, *doll*, *don*, *dock*, and so on (**serial** processing)? Or would all the possibilities be considered subsconsciously at the same time (**parallel** processing)?

The human mind, it appears, prefers the second method, that of parallel-processing, so much so that even unlikely possibilities are probably considered subconsciously. A recent **spreading activation** theory suggests that the mind is an enormously powerful network in which any work which at all resembles the one heard is automatically activated, and that each of these triggers its own neighbours, so that activation gradually spreads like ripples on a pond. Words that seem particularly appropriate get more and more excited, and those which are irrelevant gradually fade away. Eventually, one candidate wins out over the others.

Understanding syntax

We now know quite a lot about word recognition. But it is still unclear how separate words are woven together into the overall pattern.

To some extent, the process is similar to word recognition, in that people look for outline clues, and then actively reconstruct the probable message from them. In linguistic terminology, hearers utilize **perceptual strategies**—short cuts in which they impose what they expect to hear onto the stream of sounds which reaches their ear. For example, consider the sentence:

The boy kicked the ball threw it.

Most people who hear this sentence feel that there is something wrong with it, that there is a word left out somewhere, and that it would preferably be:

The boy who kicked the ball threw it.
The boy kicked the ball, then threw it.

However, they realize that it is in fact perfectly well-formed when shown a similar sentence:

> *The boy thrown the ball kicked it.* (The boy to whom the ball was thrown kicked it.)

The problem arose because when interpreting sentences, people tend to impose a subject-verb-object sequence on them. It is hard to counteract this tendency, and accounts for a number of 'garden-path' sentences, situations in which hearers are initially led 'up the garden path' in their interpretation, before realizing they have made a mistake, as in:

> *Anyone who cooks ducks out of the washing-up.*

(Anyone who cooks tries to avoid or ducks out of the washing-up).

In other cases, however, people's interpretation varies depending on the lexical items. In:

> *Clever girls and boys go to university.*

people usually assume that *clever* refers both to girls and boys. But in:

> *Small dogs and cats do not need much exercise.*

small is usually taken to refer to the dogs alone.

The relationship between lexical items, the syntax, and the overall context therefore is still under discussion. A further problem is that of 'gaps', situations in which a word has been brought to the front of the sentence, and left a 'gap' after the verb, as in:

> *Which wombat did Bill put in the cage?*

Do hearers mentally store *which wombat* until they find the place in the sentence which it slots into (in this case, after the verb *put*)? Or what happens? This matter is still hotly disputed.

Speech production

Speech production involves at least two types of process. On the one hand, words have to be selected. On the other, they have to be assembled together with the syntax.

Slips of the tongue—cases in which the speaker accidentally says something such as *par cark* instead of 'car park'—provide useful clues to these processes, and so do pauses: they can tell us where a speaker stops to think—though it is difficult to separate out pauses caused by searching for lexical items, and pauses due to syntactic planning.

There are two main kinds of slips: on the one hand, there are **selection errors**, cases in which a speaker has picked out the wrong item, as in:

*Please hand me the **tin-opener*** (nut-crackers).
*Your seat's in the third **component*** (compartment).

On the other hand, there are **assemblage errors**, cases in which a correct choice has been made, but the utterance has been wrongly assembled:

Dinner** is being served at **wine (Wine is being served at dinner).
*A **poppy** of my **caper*** (A copy of my paper).

At first sight, such slips may seem haphazard and confused. On closer inspection, they show certain regularities, so much so that some people have talked about tongue slip 'laws'—though this is something of an exaggeration. We are dealing with recurring probabilities, rather than any real kind of 'law'.

Selection errors usually involve lexical items, so they can tell us which words are closely associated in the mind. For example, people tend to say *knives* for 'forks', *oranges* for 'lemons', *left* for 'right', suggesting that words on the same general level of detail are tightly linked, especially if they are thought of as a pair. Similar sounding words which get confused tend to have similar beginnings and endings, and a similar rhythm, as in *antidote* for 'anecdote', *confusion* for 'conclusion'.

These observations were possibly first made by the two Harvard psychologists who devised a now famous 'tip of the tongue' experiment, first carried out over 20 years ago. The experimenters assembled a number of students, and read them out definitions of relatively uncommon words. For example, 'A navigational instrument used in measuring angular distances, especially the altitude of sun, moon and stars at sea'. Some of the students were unable to write down the word *sextant* immediately. The word was on the tip of their tongue, but they could not quite remember it. Those in a 'tip of the tongue state' were asked to fill in a questionnaire about their mental search. They found that they could provide quite a lot of information about the elusive word. They could often say how many syllables it had, what the first letter was, and sometimes, how it ended. They could think up similar-meaning words such as *astrolabe*, *compass*, and also similar-sounding words such as *secant*, *sexton, sextet*. This suggests that adults store and select words partly on the basis of rhythm, partly by remembering how they begin and end.

A considerable number of selection errors tend to be similar both in sound and meaning, as in *component* for 'compartment', *geraniums* for 'hydrangeas'. This suggests that a spreading activation theory, of the type proposed for speech recognition, may also be relevant in speech production. The mind activates all similar words, and those that have two kinds of similarity, both meaning and sound get more highly activated than the others, and so are more likely to pop up in error.

Whereas selection errors tell us how individual words are stored and selected, assemblage errors indicate how whole sequences are organized ready for production. For example, mistakes nearly always take place within a single 'tone group'—a short stretch of speech spoken with a single intonation contour. This suggests that the tone group is the unit of planning. And within the tone group, we note that items with similar stress are often transposed, as in

*A **gas** of **tank*** (a tank of gas).

Furthermore, when sounds are switched, initial sounds change place with other initials, and final with final, and so on, as in

Reap of hubbish (heap of rubbish).
Hass or grash (hash or grass).

All this suggests that speech is organized in accordance with a rhythmic principle—that a tone group is divided into smaller units (usually called feet), which are based (in English) on stress. Feet are divided into syllables, which are in turn possibly controlled by a biological 'beat' which regulates the speed of utterance. The interaction between these rhythmically based tone groups and syntactic constructions is a topic which still needs to be carefully examined.

QUESTIONS

1 What is meant by **maturationally controlled behaviour**?
2 What is the **content-process** controversy?
3 Child language is **rule-governed**. Explain this statement.
4 What are **perceptual strategies**?
5 How might a psycholinguist find out about sentence production?

PART FOUR

Changes and Comparisons

Change and decay in all around we see. But not all change is decay, and some decay turns into new life.

D. J. ENRIGHT

12

Language Change

All languages are continually changing—their sounds, their syntax, and their meaning. This gradual alteration is mostly unnoticed by the speakers of a language, since the sounds and syntax in particular give a superficial impression of being static. Yet one glance at the works of Chaucer or Shakespeare shows how much English has changed in a relatively short time.

A closer look at the English of today reveals several sounds and constructions in the process of changing. [j], the *y*-like sound which occurs before [uː] in words such as *tune*, *muse*, *duty* seems to be dropping out. It has already disappeared in words such as *rule*, *lute*. Soon, it may have dropped out entirely, as it has in East Anglia.

Meanwhile, a change in syntax is occurring in the use of the pronouns *I* and *me*. It used to be considered correct to say *It's I*. Nowadays, the majority of people say *It's me*. *Me* tends to be used after the verb, and *I* before it. And there are signs that this rule is being extended so that *I* occurs only in a position directly preceding the verb. The line in the popular song, 'Me and the elephant, we still remember you', is only partially a joke. Such sentences possibly encapsulate this changing rule of grammar.

People working on this branch of linguistics are interested above all in how and why language changes. They are also interested in reconstructing an earlier state of affairs in cases where we have no written records of the previous stages of the language.

How language changes

Until relatively recently, language change was considered to be a mysterious, unobservable phenomenon which crept up on one unawares. Like the movement of the planets, it was regarded as undetectable by the unaided human senses. However, advances in sociolinguistics have led to a growing understanding of the mechanisms behind both the spread of change from person to person, and its dissemination through a language.

The American sociolinguist William Labov was one of the first people to examine in detail how a change spreads through a population. He found a new pronunciation creeping in among the permanent inhabitants on the island of Martha's Vineyard, a popular holiday resort off the coast of Massachusetts. Judging by previous accounts of the islanders' speech, the vowel sounds in words such as *I*, *my* and *out*, *about* were altering their character, being produced with the mouth considerably less wide open than the standard American pronunciation. Labov did a survey of these vowels sounds, interviewing the islanders, and asking them to read passages containing the crucial words.

He found that the change seemed to be radiating out from a group of fishermen who were regarded as typifying the old true values of the island, in contrast to the despised summer visitors. The fishermen's speech had always been somewhat different from the standard American pronunciation, though in recent years, it appeared to have become more extreme. The non-standard vowels were being picked up and imitated in particular by people aged 30–45 who had made a firm decision to stay permanently on the island.

The fishermen's strange vowels, then, were not a totally new invention, they were simply an exaggeration of existing vowels. Other inhabitants who came into contact with these respected old fishermen perhaps subconsciously imitated aspects of their speech in an effort to sound like 'true' islanders. At first, the adopted fisherman-type vowels fluctuated with their existing more standard vowels, then gradually the new ones took over. At this point, the change started to spread to others who came into contact with this second group, and so on.

There is some truth, therefore, in the notion that changes are infectious. Parents sometimes complain that their children 'pick up' dreadful accents at school. But children are not infected against their will. Subconsciously at least, humans imitate those they admire, or desire to be associated with. It is as impossible to stop children acquiring the accents of their friends as it is to stop them wanting to wear the same clothes, or admiring the same pop stars.

Some changes occur 'from above', meaning 'from above the level of consciousness', when people consciously imitate the accent of others. For example, in British English, someone who comes from an area where [h] is omitted at the beginning of words such as *hot*, *high*, might make a decision to gradually incorporate it, to fit in with the more usual pronunciation. Other changes are 'from below', meaning 'from below the level of consciousness', as with the Martha's Vineyard changes, where those involved might have been unaware of which parts of their speech were changing.

But whether the changes are 'from above', or 'from below', the mechanism of spread from person to person appears to be the same: alternatives creep in, usually copied from those around, then gradually replace the existing pronunciation. Change inevitably involves variant forms while it is in progress, so speech variation is often a sign that a change is taking place.

Spread of change within a language

The spread of a change through the language is a topic which at one time seemed even more mysterious than its spread through a population. One puzzling phenomenon was the so-called 'regularity' of sound change. If one sound changes the alteration does not only occur in an isolated word. It affects all similar words in which the same sound occurs. So, in English *wyf* became *wife*, just as *lyf* became *life*, and *bryd* became *bride*, all showing a change from [iː] to [aɪ]. In the 19th century, linguists claimed that sound changes were 'laws' which worked with 'blind necessity', sweeping all before them like snow ploughs. But one problem remained. How did odd words get left behind? For example, British English [æ] normally changed into [aː] before [s], as in *pass, fast, disaster*. So why do we still get *gas, mass, aster, tassel*? It seems very puzzling that these sweeping 'laws' should rush through a language, yet somehow accidentally miss some words.

One answer was to deny that there really were any exceptions, and suggest that such words were borrowed from neighbouring dialects. For example, British [æ] in words such as *gas* might be due to American influence. But this feeble attempt to evade the problem was not really satisfactory, and recently, detailed questionnaires and surveys have revealed a better answer.

Linguists have now shown that sound changes do not occur simultaneously in all words at once. They move across the language going from one word to another, like apples on a tree, which ripen round about the same time, but not simultaneously. When charted on a diagram, the progress of the change shows a characteristic S-curve: the time scale goes along the bottom, the number of words

Fig. 50

affected up the side. First, the change touches relatively few words, and affects them variably in that the new pronunciation is likely to exist alongside the old. In the Martha's Vineyard vowels, for example, the word *I* was affected early, but the 'new' pronunciation of *I* did not happen each time, only sometimes. At this point, the change is merely a mild tendency which could be reversed, or even fade out all together. The words affected early are sometimes the commonest, but phonetic factors are also important: words beginning with vowels tended to be the most affected in Martha's Vineyard. So *I* and *out* were changed early partly because they are common words, partly because of their linguistic shape.

The early stage of a change, with just a few words intermittently affected may last a long time. But, at some point, the change is likely to 'catch on'. It will in all probability then spread fairly fast to a considerable amount of vocabulary, as shown by the steep part of the S in Figure 50. Towards the end, a change tends to lose its impetus and peter out, so there may be a few words it never reaches. This scenario, then, of a change creeping from word to word accounts for why changes are for the most part regular, but why some words can get left out. The process is known as **lexical diffusion**. The words affected by a change fluctuate at first, with the new and old pronunciation coexisting. But eventually, the newer pronunciation wins out.

Causes of language change

'There is no more reason for language to change than for jackets to have three buttons one year and two the next', asserted one well-known linguist, arguing that all change is due to accidental, social factors. This viewpoint cannot be correct, for two reasons. First, surprisingly similar changes recur the world over. There are certain tendencies inherent in language, which possibly get triggered by social factors, but which are there waiting in the wings as it were, for something to set them off, as with an avalanche: a lone skier who disturbed the snow was perhaps the immediate trigger, but there were deeper underlying causes which already existed, before that skier arrived.

Furthermore, language patterning never breaks down. This is the other reason why changes cannot be simply accidental. The patterns within language enable the mind to handle large amounts of linguistic information without strain. If change was random, the organization would break down. The mind would be overloaded with a junk-heap of disorganized information, and communication would be impossible.

These factors provide two major causes of change: on the one hand, there are underlying tendencies in language, tendencies which can get triggered by social factors. On the other hand, there is a therapeutic tendency, a tendency to make readjustments in order to restore broken patterns. Let us briefly consider these.

Natural tendencies

There are numerous natural tendencies, and some of them are stronger than others. They can be triggered by social factors, or may be held at bay for centuries, perhaps held in check by other opposing tendencies.

A widespread tendency is for the ends of words to disappear. In cases where this has largely occurred already, as in the Polynesian languages, Italian, and French, many English speakers claim the language 'sounds beautiful', 'has flowing sounds'. But when it begins to happen to our own language, and people leave [t] off the end of words such as *hot*, *what*, and replace it with a 'glottal stop'— a closure at the back of the vocal tract with no actual sound emitted—then many people get upset, and talk about 'sloppiness', and 'disgraceful swallowing of sounds'. However, such an incident is certainly not 'sloppiness', since producing a glottal stop requires as much muscular tension as the sound it replaces. Furthermore, the change is creeping in inexorably: even those who criticize it usually fail to notice that they themselves are likely to replace [t] with a glottal stop in *football*, *hot milk*, *a bit more*. In some areas, the change has affected [k] as well, and also, to a lesser extent, [p]. At the rate at which it seems to be spreading, [p], [t] and [k] may have disappeared from the end of British English words by the middle of the next century.

Not all tendencies are major, noticeable ones. Others can be minor, affecting only one sound in a particular position: the sound [e] tends to become [i] before [ŋ], so *England* is now pronounced as if it were spelled 'Ingland'. A [b] tends to be inserted between [m] and [l], so the word *bramble* is from an earlier *bremel*. And so on.

Some tendencies can have repercussions throughout the language, as with the loss of the ends of words, which means that in French, for example, an alternative means of expressing 'plural' has had to be developed: it is essential to put *les* [le] at the beginning of plural words, as in *les chats* [le ʃa] 'the cats', since by itself the word for 'cat' [ʃa] is pronounced the same in both the singular and plural: this distinction is now marked by the determiner placed in front of it.

Therapeutic changes

Therapeutic changes restore patterns which have been damaged by previous changes. A number of examples of this are provided by the use of **analogy**, the ability to reason from parallel cases, which is a fundamental feature of human language. It is most obvious in the case of child language, when children form plurals such as *mans*, *mouses*, *foots*, after hearing plurals such as *cats*, *dogs*, *horses*.

In language change, analogy tends to restore similar forms to items which have become separated by sound changes. For example, changes in the vowel system resulted in the separation of the adjective *old* from its comparative form *elder*. So a new comparative form *older* has been formed by analogy with forms such as *young*, *younger*, where the first part of both words is the same. The form *elder* has now been relegated to a few specialized uses and phrases, such as *elders of the church*, *his elder brother*.

However, it is a mistake to regard analogy purely as a restorer of broken patterns. This is an oversimplification, because analogy is not only found in a therapeutic role: it can itself disrupt sound changes. For example, we would expect [d] in the middle of the word *father* (as in Gothic *fadar*). But *father* was influenced by the word *brother*, and the expected [d] appears as [ð]. In addition, there are a number of different types of analogy. In some ways, it is a 'rag-bag' category used to explain a variety of changes. So it is misleading to make vague general claims about analogy, unless we can narrow down our statement to one particular type.

Changes which trigger one another off

Chain shifts—that is, changes which seem to occur in linked sequences—are a particularly interesting therapeutic phenomenon. For example, in Chaucer's time the word *lyf* 'life' was pronounced [liːf] (like today's *leaf*). The vowel [iː] changed to [eɪ] (and later to [aɪ]). But this was not an isolated change. At around this time, all the other long vowels shifted: [eː] became [iː] [ɛː] became [eː], and [aː] became [ɛː]. It looks as if each vowel rushed to fill the empty space left by the one ahead of it (Figure 51).

Fig. 51

Yet the situation is not necessarily as straightforward as the example given here—which is itself disputed. Quite often, several sounds move simultaneously, making it difficult to say whether one sound is being dragged into an empty space, or whether it is being pushed out of its rightful place. In Figure 52, is [eː] being dragged into the space left by [iː]? Or is it being pushed by [ɛː]? Controversy surrounds the actual mechanism by which sounds affect one another. The only certain fact is that changes seem to occur in linked sequences, and in so doing preserve the basic patterning of human language.

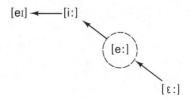

Fig. 52

Recently, linguists have suggested that chain shifts occur not only in the sounds of a language, but in the syntax also. For example, some languages have relative clauses (clauses introduced by *which*, *that*) placed before the nouns attached to them. They say, as it were,

Which is sour wine

where English says 'Wine which is sour'. Such languages also tend to have objects which precede their verbs. A literal translation of English 'Harry dislikes wine which is sour' might be

Harry [which is sour wine] dislikes.

If, however, a change occurs so that relative clauses move to a position after their nouns, then the verb and object are likely to change places also. Once again, most people would agree that the changes are linked in some way, though the precise mechanism is disputed.

Interacting changes

So far, the changes examined have been fairly straightforward. But some types of change are far more complex. In order to give some idea of the numerous factors normally involved in a language change, let us finally look at some *interacting* changes. In the following example, loss of word endings has combined with changes in word order, to bring about both the disappearance of a construction and a change of meaning.

The forerunner of the English word *like* was *lician*, a verb which meant 'to give pleasure to'. This verb was in common use in English at a time when objects normally preceded the verb, and the subject of the sentence did not necessarily come at the beginning of a sentence. A typical sentence might be:

tham	*cynge*	*licodon*	*peran*
to the	king	gave pleasure	pears

'Pears pleased the king'.

Then, over the course of several centuries, two things happened. First, the noun and verb endings were dropped. *The king* became the standard form for the noun, and the plural ending dropped from the verb. This eventually led to the form:

The king liked pears.

Meanwhile, it gradually became normal to put the subject before the verb, and the object after it. So the sentence 'The king liked pears', which originally meant 'To the king were a pleasure pears', was reinterpreted as 'The king took pleasure in pears'. Therefore, loss of word endings and a word order change have triggered off two further changes: the loss of the construction-type 'to someone, something is a pleasure', and a change of meaning in the word *like* from 'to give pleasure to' to 'to take pleasure in'. This example illustrates the fact that, in most types of language change, a multiplicity of factors are involved.

Reconstruction

Recently, an enormous amount has been found out about language change by examining changes in progress. However, language change is a relatively slow process, so we need in addition to consider how languages have altered over the centuries. Yet our written records are inevitably incomplete. In order to supplement these, historical linguists extend their knowledge by reconstructing stages of language for which there are no written documents.

There are a number of different types of reconstruction. The best known of these is **external reconstruction**, also known as **comparative historical linguistics**. In this, a linguist compares the forms of words in genetically related languages, that is, languages which have developed from some common source, and then draws conclusions about their common ancestor. This type of reconstruction will be discussed further in Chapter 13. An older name for it is 'comparative philology', which sometimes causes confusion, since in the USA, France and Germany, 'philology' normally refers to the study of literary texts.

A second type of reconstruction is known as **internal reconstruction**. In this, linguists look at the state of one language at a single point in time. By comparing elements which are likely to have had a common origin, they are often able to draw conclusions about their earlier form. To take a simple example, consider the words *long* and *longer*. /lɒŋ/ and /lɒŋg/ (with /g/ on the end) are both allomorphs of the morpheme *long*. This suggests that, originally, they were identical, and that the word *long* was once pronounced with [g] at the end (as it still is in some parts of England, such as Liverpool).

A third type of reconstruction is **typological reconstruction**. This is somewhat newer than the other two. Linguists are beginning to be able to divide languages into different types, and to recognize the basic characteristics attached to each type; this branch of linguistics is known as language typology. For example, those languages (such as Hindi) which have verbs after their objects, also tend to have auxiliary verbs after the main verb. On the other hand, languages such as English which have verbs before their objects tend to have auxiliary verbs before the main verb. If, therefore, we were to find the remnants of a language which had its auxiliaries attached after the main verb, we would be able to predict that it might also have its object before the verb, even if we had no direct evidence for this. Typology will be discussed further in Chapter 13.

Let us now see how we might use these three types of reconstruction. Suppose we have three related languages, Twiddle, Twuddle and Twoddle. Let us also assume that we have no past records, merely a record of their present-day speech. First, we would use internal reconstruction (IR) to reconstruct an earlier state of each of these languages—Early Twiddle, Early Twuddle and Early Twoddle. Then we would use external reconstruction (ER) to reconstruct Proto-T, the common ancestor of these three. Then, once again, we would employ internal reconstruction, this time combined with typological reconstruction (TR) to reconstruct an earlier form of Proto-T: Pre-Proto-T (Figure 53).

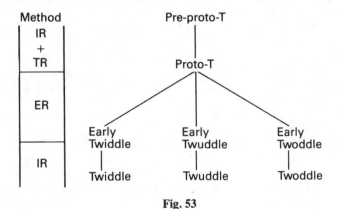

Fig. 53

In this way, we might be able to reconstruct a probable history of these languages stretching over hundreds, and perhaps even thousands of years.

QUESTIONS

1 How do changes spread from person to person?
2 How do changes spread within a language?
3 Suggest two types of causes of language change.
4 What is **analogy**?
5 What is a **chain shift**?
6 Name three types of **reconstruction**, and explain in outline what each involves.

13

Comparing Languages

Estimates as to the number of different languages in the world vary considerably, partly because of problems in defining the word 'language' (Chapter 11). The figure most usually quoted is somewhere between 4,000 and 8,000. A few linguists carry out detailed studies of individual languages. Many more, however, are involved in comparing pairs or groups of them. Sometimes they compare them in order to pinpoint dissimilarities (**contrastive linguistics**) and sometimes to identify similarities, which may be due to **universal**, **genetic**, **areal** or **typological** factors.

Contrastive linguistics

The comparison of languages in order to find dissimilarities is known as **contrastive linguistics**. It is carried out mainly by **applied linguists**, the name usually given to people who look at the application of linguistic principles to the field of language teaching. It is useful to know in advance where someone learning a language is likely to have difficulties, and these often arise in areas of the 'target' language which are very different from one's own. For example, in Hindi, negation is very simple for the most part. A single negative word is placed before the verb, which is at the end of the sentence:

Bill hindustani nahī hai.
Bill – Indian – not – is
'Bill is not Indian'.

Because of this, Indian learners of English often have difficulties with the English preference for bringing negatives to the front, and they tend to produce sentences such as:

All of these pens don't work.

where a British English speaker would prefer:

None of these pens work.

Constrastive linguists, therefore, make detailed comparisons of pairs of languages in order to pinpoint dissimilarities. This enables them to predict difficulties likely to be experienced by learners, which will in turn influence the preparation of teaching materials.

Language similarities

In a broad sense, almost all linguists are looking for language similarities, since the search for language universals is one of the major tasks of linguistics (Chapters 14–16). Many linguists, however, study characteristics shared by groups of languages, rather than all of them. **Genetic**, **areal** and **typological** factors are the three main causes behind these shared features. Genetically-based similarities occur when languages are descended from a common ancestor. Areally-based similarities are due to contact between neighbouring languages. And typologically-based similarities occur when languages belong to the same overall 'type'. Let us look at each of these.

Genetic similarities

The search for genetically related languages, and the reconstruction of the hypothetical parent language from which they were descended, was considered to be the most important task of linguistics in the nineteenth century (Chapter 3). These days, comparative historical linguistics is a branch of historical linguistics (Chapter 12). It enables us to follow through the development of a language from an early stage, and to distinguish inherited features from recent innovations.

It is often not immediately apparent which languages are related. At first glance, Welsh, Spanish and Russian look quite different, yet these are all Indo-European languages. We need to look for systematic correspondences between the languages, rather than similar-looking words, which can be misleading. For example, it is mere chance that German *haben* 'have' resembles Latin *habere* 'have'. And Turkish *plaz* 'beach' only sounds like French *plage* 'beach' because it was borrowed from French. On the other hand, *beef* and *cow* are (perhaps surprisingly) related, and so are the words *paradise*, *dough* and *fiction*, which can be traced back to a Proto-Indo European word meaning 'make, mould, build'.

Two basic assumptions underlie our search for systematic correspondences. First, linguistic symbols are essentially arbitrary. As explained in Chapter 2, there is no connection between the sound of a word and the thing it symbolizes, except in the case of occasional onomatopoeic words. Therefore consistent similarities between languages which cannot be explained by borrowing may be due to common origin. The second assumption is that sound changes are for the most part regular. If one sound changes, then all similar sounds in the same phonetic environment and geographical area change also. On the basis of these two assumptions, we may draw up reliable and systematic correspondences between the various related languages.

The correspondences which we look for can be found either in the sounds, or, more reliably, in the morphology, since it is rare (though not impossible) for one language to borrow another's morphology. Figure 54 shows some English and German examples:

German			English
/d/			/θ/
dick	fat	←——→	**th**ick
Ding	thing	←——→	**th**ing
Ba**d**	bath	←——→	ba**th**

/ʃv/			/sw/
schwimmen	swim	←——→	**sw**im
schwingen	swing	←——→	**sw**ing
Schwan	swan	←——→	**sw**an

Fig. 54

These systematic sound correspondences between words with the same or similar meaning are the first clue that the languages may be related. The evidence is cumulative. The more correspondences, the more likely the languages are to be related. In the German–

English examples above, the words are fairly similar, but (as already noted) this is not essential. For example, we can recognize the relationship between English and Latin on the basis of correspondences between words such as

| Latin *pater* 'father' | English *father* |
| *pes* 'foot' | *foot* |

Here Latin *p* consistently corresponds to English *f*.

However, correspondences must never be accepted uncritically. We might be dealing with a series of loanwords which diverged in development after being borrowed. For example, there is a superficial correspondence between

French *mouton* 'sheep'	English *mutton*
bouton 'button'	*button*
glouton 'glutton'	*glutton*

But these are all words borrowed from French at the time of the Norman invasion. More reliable are morphological correspondences, such as that shown in Figure 55.

German

No suffix	/ə/	/ste/
klein	klein**er**	klein**ste**
schnell	schnell**er**	schnell**ste**
reich	reich**er**	reich**ste**

English

No suffix	/ə/	/est/
small	small**er**	small**est**
quick	quick**er**	quick**est**
rich	rich**er**	rich**est**

Fig. 55

Such correspondences definitely prove that German and English are related. And earlier in this century, Hittite was established as an Indo-European language on the basis of morphological correspondences, in spite of the fact that its vocabulary consists mainly of non-Indo-European words.

Building a family tree

Once we have established that a number of languages are related, then we have to form a hypothesis as to exactly how they are linked. If we find three related or 'cognate' languages, say German, English and French, then we have to decide whether they should form three separate branches from the parent, or whether (as is in fact the case) two of them diverged from one another at a later stage (Figure 56).

Fig. 56

This would affect our reconstruction, because we would then have to reconstruct the ancestor of German and English before moving on to the next stage, that of reconstructing the overall ancestor.

Reconstructing the parent language

When we have set up a family tree, we can begin to reconstruct. We do this by looking first of all at the 'majority verdict'. That is, we look at the sounds found in daughter languages of a similar age, and, as a first hypothesis, suggest that those on which the majority agree might represent the original sounds. For example, among the Indo-European languages, we find Sanskrit *sapta*, Greek *hepta*, Latin *septem*, all meaning 'seven'. This group of words suggest that the parent language word was perhaps [septa].

Second, our preliminary hypothesis must be checked to see if the developments we have proposed are phonetically probable. We are assuming, for example, that in Greek, [s] changed to [h], that in Sanskrit, [e] changed to [a], and that in Latin [a] changed to [em]. Are such changes possible or likely? In this case, the answer is 'yes' as far as [s]→[h], and [e]→[a] are concerned, but 'no' to [a]→ [em], which is highly unlikely. [em]→[a] would be more probable. Can we propose an original [septem]?

On checking further, we discover that Greek and Sanskrit do not normally lose all trace of [m] at the end of words, so something must be wrong somewhere. A more plausible hypothesis is that the final syllable was originally rather like the sound sometimes heard at the end of English *madam*, in which [m] appears to be behaving in a vowel-like manner. This vowel-like [m] (sometimes written [m̩]) commonly becomes either [a] or [em], so our final reconstruction for the word 'seven' is [septm̩].

As we gradually build up a picture of the proto-language, we need in addition to check whether, in the light of our knowledge of languages in general, we have reconstructed a possible proto-language. If it looks totally unlike any language we have ever seen, then we should be suspicious of our conclusions.

Unreliability of reconstructions

It is, unfortunately, most unlikely that we shall succeed in reconstructing an accurate representation of the parent language. For a start, there are always enormous gaps in the evidence available. In the reconstruction of Proto-Indo-European, linguists rely overmuch on Greek, Latin and Sanskrit because of the extensive written records which have survived. Similar written records of Albanian or Armenian might dramatically change the picture. Second, it is not always possible to deduce the actual pronunciation from written texts, yet our reconstructions are to a large extent based on these texts. Third, no parent language is ever a single, homogeneous whole. Every language has dialectal variations within it, so reconstructions are likely to be hotch-potch forms made up from several dialects. Fourth, daughter languages sometimes undergo independent, parallel developments which can falsify the picture of the parent language. If we possessed only English, Russian and Italian, we might wrongly deduce that Indo-European had a stress accent. But stress developed independently in all three languages after the break-up of the parent language. Fifth, borrowing from neighbours can distort the picture.

In conclusion, we realize that reconstructions merely represent the best guesses we can make about the parent language in the light of current knowledge. No one nowadays has the confidence of the 19th-century scholar who attempted to translate one of Aesop's fables into Proto-Indo-European! Their main value is that they allow us to distinguish possible inherited features in a language from those which are recent innovations, and to extend our knowledge of the history of languages.

Linguistic areas

When similarities are found between adjacent languages, so-called **borrowing** should be suspected as a possible source. Languages which come into contact with one another often take over some of the linguistic features of their neighbours. Borrowed vocabulary items are particulary common: English has adopted numerous French food words: *courgettes*, *aubergines*, *pâté*, for example. Borrowing of constructions is more likely to occur if the languages are structurally similar. But even dissimilar languages can, over time, gradually absorb features from one another. If some particularly striking characteristic has spread over a wide range, linguists sometimes talk about 'linguistic areas'.

The reason for studying areal characteristics is twofold: on the one hand, knowledge of how languages can affect one another extends our understanding of language change. On the other hand, it is important to isolate shared features caused by borrowing, so as not to confuse them with genetic and typological similarities.

Areal features can involve any aspect of the language. For example, Chinese, Thai and Vietnamese are all spoken in the Far East, and they are all tone languages, something which has apparently come about through contact. And in India, languages with quite different origins have all developed a particular type of sound, known as a 'retroflex', in which the tongue is curled backwards against the palate.

Several Balkan languages show similarities which appear to be due to proximity. Albanian, Bulgarian and Romanian all have the so-called 'definite article' *the* attached after the noun. For example, Romanian has *munte-le* 'mountain-the', a construction which has clearly been borrowed from its neighbours, since languages to which it is more closely related show the reverse order, as in the historically related French equivalent *le mont* 'the mount'. The same three languages, as well as another neighbour, modern Greek, all say the equivalent of: 'Give me that I eat', when one might have expected them to say: 'Give me to eat', judging from other European languages. These particular features seem to have spread during the centuries when Byzantine culture was a unifying force in this part of the world.

Language types

Parallel structures in languages may occur because the languages are of a similar type. Just as one can divide human beings into different racial types on the basis of characteristics such as bone structure, skin colour, blood group and so on, so one can divide languages into different groups.

The recent interest in **linguistic typology** has arisen in part out of the failure to find large numbers of language universals. Absolute universals, characteristics shared by all languages, proved to be hard to identify, and those attempting to list them were driven back onto vague statements such as: 'All languages have the means of asking questions'. When people tried to pin these statements down further, such as querying *how* questions were asked, it became clear that certain devices recurred in human languages, though different languages favoured different constructions.

Of course, the observation that different languages use different constructions is by no means new. What is new, is the recent interest in **implicational universals** and implicational tendencies. That is, if a language has a particular construction, it is also likely to have further predictable characteristics. Just as one one can say that, if an animal has feathers and a beak, it is also likely to have wings, so one can make statements of the type: 'If a language has a basic pattern of subject, verb, object, it is also likely to have prepositions (rather than postpositions)'.

Morphological criteria for language classification

What criteria should form the basis for language classification? There is considerable controversy about this. The earliest work on the topic, in the last century, was based on the way in which morphemes were handled.

The number of morphemes per word varies from language to language—so does the way in which morphemes are combined within a word. In the 19th century, scholars tried to use such criteria for dividing languages into different types. They recognized at least *three* different morphological types.

An **isolating** (or analytical) language is one in which words frequently consist of one morpheme. This is often the case in English:

Will you please let the dog out now.

An **agglutinating** language (from the Latin word for 'glue together') is one in which words can be divided into morphemes without difficulty. Turkish and Swahili are well-known examples. But agglutination is also used to a limited extent in English:

lov-ing-ly   faith-ful-ness

A **fusional** language is one such as Latin which fuses morphemes together in such a way that they are not easily recognizable as separate elements. For example, *-us* on the end of *taurus* 'bull' indicates that it is masculine, singular, and the subject of the sentence, but these three aspects cannot be disentangled. Occasional examples of fusion occur in English:

went = go + past tense

At one time it was thought that languages followed a fixed pattern of development. The first stage was an isolating one, the second agglutinating, the third fusional. Greek and Latin were spoken of in sentimental terms as representing the highest and best of language types. Everything else was regarded as an aberration, or a symptom of decline and decay. The fallacy of such a belief is pointed out vividly by the American anthropologist and linguist Edward Sapir: 'A linguist that insists on talking about the Latin type of morphology as though it were necessarily the high-water mark of linguistic development is like the zoologist that sees in the organic world a huge conspiracy to evolve the race-horse or the Jersey cow.'

The main flaw in the type of classification outlined above is that no language is a 'pure' morphological type. A few languages fit into one category rather than another, but many appear to have mixed morphological processes. So nowadays, most linguists use other criteria for dividing languages into different types.

Word order criteria

English uses word order as a basic syntactic device. In linguistic terminology, it is a **configurational language** (Chapter 7). Perhaps for this reason there has been an enormous amount of interest in word order as a typological characteristic. Among the possible word orders, only a limited number are commonly used, and each of these is likely to possess certain predictable characteristics.

The most usual preliminary classification is in terms of subject, verb, object. In theory, there are six possibilities:

Subject first	*Verb first*	*Object first*
SOV	VSO	OVS
SVO	VOS	OSV

In practice, the ones on the left (subject first) are considerably more common than the ones in the middle (verb first), whereas the ones on the right (object first) are extremely rare. In fact, no sure example of OSV has ever been found, and the few examples of OVS are clustered together in South America.

Examples of languages which fit each of these types, with the literal order in which they would express a sentence *The dog killed the duck* are:

SOV *The dog the duck killed* (Turkish).
SVO *The dog killed the duck* (English).
VSO *Killed the dog the duck* (Welsh).
VOS *Killed the duck the dog* (Malagasy (Madagascar)).
OVS *The duck killed the dog* (Hixkaryana (S. America)).
OSV *The duck the dog killed* (??).

This preliminary classification is useful, but it also presents a number of problems. The most obvious difficulty is that there are a number of languages which do not fit easily into one of these categories, for various reasons. In some languages, such as the Australian languages Dyirbal and Walbiri, it seems to be impossible to identify a 'basic' word order. These appear to be genuine non-configurational languages: their word order is extremely free and flexible. In other languages, the word order seems to be fixed, but mixed. For example, German has SVO order in main clauses, but SOV in subordinate clauses. It says in effect:

The dog killed the duck (SVO, main clause).
I heard that [the dog the duck killed] (SOV, subordinate clause).

Furthermore, in several languages, it is extremely difficult to identify the 'subject' of the verb. Take the sentences:

The dog killed the duck.
The dog ran away.

In English, *the dog* would be regarded as the subject of both these sentences. But in some languages, such as Eskimo, *the duck* in the first sentence would be given the same inflectional ending as *the dog* in the second sentence. Situations such as this make it difficult to make reliable decisions about what is a 'subject', and what is an 'object'. The rationale behind the Eskimo situation (somewhat simplified) is that there is a standard ending put on most nouns, but this is changed in cases where there are two nouns in a sentence, in which case the more active participant the 'agent', is given a special ending.

In addition, so-called **pro-drop** languages cause problems. These are languages which omit the subject of a sentence when it is a pronoun. In Latin, for example, *cano* 'sing-I' was commoner than *ego cano* 'I sing-I', where the pronoun was added only if extra emphasis was needed. In these languages, the order of verb and object when the pronoun is dropped is not necessarily the same as that of verb and object when S,V,O are all present.

These problems show that word order classifications are not entirely trustworthy. However, statistically, certain probabilities emerge. For example: an SVO language is likely to have auxiliaries preceding the verb, prepositions rather than postpositions, and genitives following the noun, whereas an SOV language is likely to have auxiliary verbs after the verb, postpositions rather than prepositions, and genitives preceding the noun. The English examples on the left would be likely to be represented in an SOV language by the order on the right:

SVO	*Bill eats potatoes.*	SOV	*Bill potatoes eats.*
AUX V	*Marigold can go.*	V AUX	*Marigold go can.*
PREP	*On Saturday.*	POSTP	*Saturday on.*
N GEN	*Queen of Sheba.*	GEN N	*Of Sheba queen.*

Because language is always changing, there are very few languages which are 'pure' types, in the sense of being a perfect example of the statistical probabilities. Most languages have some inconsistencies, and some **doublets** (double possibilities). English, for example, can say *Sheba's queen* as well as *queen of Sheba*.

However, a list of statistical probabilities is only a first stage in the working out of language types. The second, and more important stage, is to find out why these probabilities exist. This is still under discussion, and there may be several interacting explanations. One suggestion is that in languages there is a **principle of cross-category harmony**. That is, different linguistic categories such as nouns, verbs and prepositions, all behave somewhat similarly to one another: the main word or **head** in a phrase is likely to be in a similar position throughout the different types of phrases. For example, if a verb normally occurs at the beginning of the verb phrase, as in English *eats peanuts*, then a preposition is likely to be at the front of its phrase, as in *on Saturday*, and an adjective at the front of its phrase, as in *red in the face*, and a noun at the front of its phrase, as in *father of the family*. Interestingly, the conclusion that languages behave in this way has also been arrived at independently by theoretical linguists trying to describe sentence patterns (X-bar syntax, Chapter 7).

Implicational probabilities can also, with a certain amount of caution, be used to reconstruct probable earlier states, as a supplement to other types of reconstruction in historical linguistics (Chapter 12). If we found traces of an old language which had verbs after objects and postpositions, then we would also be able to say that it was statistically likely to have genitives preceding nouns, for example.

At the moment, there is still an enormous amount more to be done in relation to typological characteristics for classifying languages, and the ensuing implicational relationships. Recently, Chomsky and his followers have started to take an interest in this type of work. Some of these ideas will be discussed in Chapter 16.

QUESTIONS

1 What is **contrastive linguistics**?
2 Suggest three reasons why languages might show similarities.
3 How might one recognize genetically related languages?
4 What is the purpose of reconstructing a proto-language?
5 What are **implicational universals**?
6 Which basic word orders are the commonest among the world's languages?

PART FIVE

Towards a Universal Grammar

He that understands grammar in one language, understands it in another as far as the essential properties of Grammar are concerned.

ROGER BACON

14

Seeking a Suitable Framework

Noam Chomsky is perhaps the most influential figure in 20th century linguistics. As we noted in Chapter 3, his contribution has been twofold. On the one hand, he initiated the era of **generative linguistics**, in that he directed attention towards the rules which underlie a person's knowledge of their language. Someone who knows a language is somewhat like a chess-player, who in order to play the game, has had to learn rules which specify which moves are possible, and which not. These rules crystallize the essence of the game. Similarly, the set of rules or 'grammar' underlying a language is, in Chomsky's view, of greater interest than any actual utterances a speaker happens to make.

On the other hand, Chomsky renewed people's interest in **language universals**. This topic was somewhat unfashionable in the early part of the century, when it was commonly assumed that: 'Languages differ without limit and in unpredictable ways'. Chomsky argues that linguists should concentrate not so much on finding out components which are common to all languages, which may well be few in number, but on discovering the bounds or **constraints** within which language operates.

Chomsky did not simply make vague statements about the need for generative grammars and universal constraints: he has put forward a number of detailed proposals for a universal framework. Unfortunately for those trying to come to grips with his ideas, he has changed his mind over many facets of his theory since it was first proposed in the 1950s. However, one basic characteristic of his proposed universal framework stays firm: it is essentially a **transformational** grammar. In this chapter, we will explain how he arrived at this particular type of grammar in the first place, and sketch out its main characteristics. Then we will consider why he has emended his original ideas (Chapter 15), and finally we will outline some of his more recent proposals (Chapter 16).

Simple models of grammar

Let us now assume that we are in the position that Chomsky was in several years ago—that of a linguist trying to set up a universal grammatical framework. Where should we begin? One fairly obvious way to get going is to write a grammar of a language we know, say, English. If we managed to do this adequately, we could then see to what extent our framework might be used for other languages also. In writing a grammar for English we would adopt the procedure used by all social scientists: we would make a guess or hypothesis, in this case about the rules internalized by someone who knows English. Then we would test the validity of this hypothesis by checking it against some raw data—the sentences of English. If the rules we hypothesized did not lead to good English sentences, they would have to be discarded or amended.

In doing this, we are *not* trying to model the way in which humans prepare a sentence for utterance. A grammar is above all a device which specifies what is, and what is not, a well-formed sentence. It encapsulates rules which define possible sentences, but it does not concern itself with how these possibilities are assembled.

The main task, therefore, is to write a grammar which has the same output as a human being—though there is no guarantee that it will replicate the rules in a person's mind. There will probably be some overlap between a linguist's rules and those actually internalized by human beings, but the mechanisms are unlikely to be identical.

Let us now consider how we might go about forming a hypothesis which would account for the grammar of English. Perhaps the best way is to start with a very simple hypothesis—possibly an over-simple one—and see what flaws it contains. Then, in the light of what we have learnt, we can proceed to a second, more complex hypothesis. And so on.

The simplest possible hypothesis might be to suggest that words are linked together in long chains, with each word attached to the next. For example, the determiners *the* and *a* might be linked to a set of nouns such as *camel*, *elephant*, which in turn might be linked to a set of verbs such as *swallowed, ate,* and so on (Figure 57). But we would very quickly have to abandon such a simple model. Neither English, nor any other language, works in this fashion. A word is

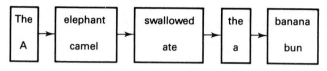

Fig. 57

not necessarily dependent on adjacent words. Often, it depends on another word that is some distance away, as in the sentence

Either *learn to play the trumpet properly* **or** *take up yoga.*
Petronella *fell and hurt* **herself**.

The *or* which is intrinsically connected to *either* appears several words away, not directly after it. Similarly, *herself* which is dependent on *Petronella* is some distance away. Another problem with the 'chain' model above is that it wrongly regards each word as attached to the next by an equal bond. The model fails to show that, in the sentence:

The camel swallowed an apple.

The words *the* and *camel* are more closely related to one another than *swallowed* and *an*. So this simple model must be abandoned.

A somewhat more satisfactory model might be one which treats sentences as if they had a 'layered' structure, as represented in the tree diagrams discussed in Chapter 7. This assumes that languages have several basic sentence patterns, each with a number of different 'slots' which can be expanded in various ways. A noun phrase (NP) followed by a verb phrase (VP) is a basic English sentence type, and this pattern can be expanded in various ways (Figure 58).

NP	VP
Ducks	bite
Ducks	bite burglars
The duck	bit the burglar

Fig. 58

Such a grammar (often called a **phrase structure** grammar) contains a series of phrase structure rules, normally in the form of rewrite rules which show the progressive expansions (as outlined in Chapter 7):

$$S \rightarrow NP \quad VP$$
$$VP \rightarrow V \quad (NP)$$
$$NP \rightarrow D \quad N$$

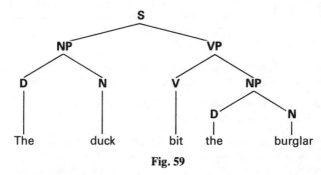

Fig. 59

There seems little doubt that some such expansion mechanism must be built into any grammar. However, according to Chomsky, such a model is incomplete. It contains at least two serious flaws. First, we require an enormous number of rules in order to generate all the sentences of English. Second, it groups together sentences which are dissimilar, and separates others which are similar. Take the sentences:

Hezekiah is anxious to help.
Hezekiah is difficult to help.

NP	V	ADJ	INF
Hezekiah	is	anxious	to help
Hezekiah	is	difficult	to help

Fig. 60

To someone who knows English, these sentences are radically different. In the first one, Hezekiah is planning to do the helping, and in the other, he is the one liable to be helped. Yet the 'slot' pattern of both is identical (Figure 60). A similar problem occurs with the sentence:

Hezekiah is ready to eat.

Any English speaker could (with a bit of thought) interpret this sentence in two ways: Hezekiah was hungry, and wanted to have his dinner. Or Hezekiah had perhaps fallen into the hands of cannibals, and had been trussed up and seasoned ready for consumption. The slot model, however, cannot easily show the two radically different interpretations of this sentence.

The reverse problem occurs with pairs of sentences such as:

To swallow safety pins is quite stupid.
It is quite stupid to swallow safety pins.

Yesterday it snowed.
It snowed yesterday.

The sentences in each pair would be regarded as very similar by English speakers, yet this similarity cannot be captured by the model of grammar outlined above, since each sentence requires a different slot pattern.

Chomsky argues that a grammar which provides only one structure for sentences which are felt to be radically different by native speakers, and different structures for sentences which are felt to be similar, is a bad grammar. A transformational model, he claims, overcomes these problems.

Deep and surface structures

Chomsky's solution to the problem was to suggest that every sentence has two levels of structure, one which is obvious on the **surface**, and another which is **deep** and abstract. Let us see how this works in connection with the sentences discussed above. Chomsky accounted for the difference between

Hezekiah is anxious to help.

and

Hezekiah is difficult to help.

by suggesting that we are dealing with sentences which have a similar **surface structure**, but different **deep structures** (Figure 61). The first would have a deep structure something like:

Hezekiah be + PRES *anxious for Hezekiah to help.*

and the second a deep structure something like:

For someone to help Hezekiah be + PRES *difficult.*

(PRES means 'present tense'. The deep structures discussed in this chapter are simplified versions of those proposed by Chomsky in his

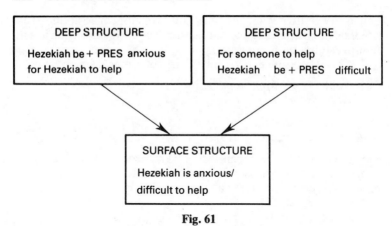

Fig. 61

so-called 'Standard Theory' of transformational grammar, outlined in his book *Aspects of the Theory of Syntax* (1965)). A similar explanation accounts for the ambiguity in:

Hezekiah was ready to eat.

where two different deep structures are realized by a single surface structure.

The situation would be reversed for pairs such as:

Yesterday it snowed.
It snowed yesterday.

Here two different surface structures share a common deep structure (Figure 62):

Fig. 62

If every sentence has two levels of structure, then it is clearly necessary to link these two levels in some way. Chomsky suggested that deep structures are related to surface structures by processes called **transformations**. A deep structure is transformed into its related surface structure by the application of one or more transformations. For example, the sentence

It snowed yesterday.

would require only one transformation—the attachment of the tense to the end of the verb. But the sentence

Yesterday it snowed.

requires a second one also, one which moves the adverb *yesterday* from the end of the sentence to the beginning.

Transformational grammar

We are now able to give a definition of a **transformational grammar**. It is a grammar which sets up two levels of structure, and relates these levels by means of operations known as **transformations**.

A transformational grammar has (like most other types of grammar) three major components: a syntactic component (dealing with syntax), a phonological component (dealing with sounds) and a semantic component (dealing with meaning). However, it differs from other grammars in that the syntactic component is split into *two* components: the **base**, and the **transformational rules** (Figure 63).

In the Standard Theory, the base contained phrase structure (PS) rules for the formation of deep structures, and also a lexicon,

Fig. 63

from which words were slotted into the output of the PS rules (Figure 64).

Fig. 64

The deep structures then passed to the transformational rules in order to be converted into the surface structures. At this point, the surface structure of a sentence was still abstract: it did not yet have a phonetic form. This was coped with by the phonological component, which converted each surface structure into a phonetic representation. Meanwhile, transformations could not change meaning, so the deep structures were fed directly into the semantic component, which gave a semantic interpretation of each (Figure 65).

Deep structure

Chomsky did not base his claim that there are two levels of structure purely on the flimsy notion of a native speaker's intuitions. There are other, more technical reasons. The most important arguments

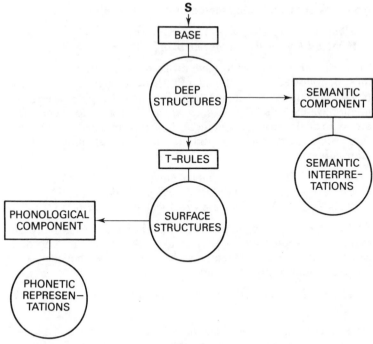

Fig. 65

are based on movement, cases in which sentence constituents appear to have been moved out of their 'proper' place. Consider the sentence:

Petronella put the parrot in a drawer.

This sentence contains the verb *put* which, as we saw in Chapter 7, has to be followed by both an NP and a PP (Figure 66):

NP	V	NP	PP
Petronella	put	the parrot	in a drawer

Fig. 66

We cannot say:

  ⋆Petronella put in the drawer.
  ⋆Petronella put the parrot.

Now look at the following sentences:

What *did Petronella put* [—] *in the drawer?*
What *did Petronella put the parrot in* [—]?

These sentences appear to have broken the requirement that *put* must be followed by an NP and a PP. Instead, *what* appears at the beginning of the sentence, and there is a gap in the place where one might have expected a word such as *parrot*, *drawer* to occur. How are we to deal with these sentences? One possibility is to complicate the lexical entry for *put*, and to say that *put* allows several alternatives:

NP *put* NP PP (*Petronella put the parrot in the drawer.*)
What NP *put* PP (*What did Petronella put in the drawer?*)
What NP *put* NP P (*What did Petronella put the parrot in?*)

Such extra additions to the lexical entry would eventually get extremely complicated, as they would have to take into account cases in which extra sub-sentences had been added between *what* and the original sentence, as in:

What *[did you say] [the police alleged] Petronella had put in the drawer?*

Of course, if the verb *put* was the only lexical item which allowed such manipulations to occur, one might simply put up with this one huge and messy lexical entry. But every verb that is normally followed by an NP allows similar contortions:

Felix grabbed the canary.
What *did Felix grab?*
What *[did Angela claim] Felix grabbed?*

Because of the generality of this occurrence—leaving a 'gap' where an NP was expected, and putting *what* in front of the sentence, it seems more plausible to conclude that it is a general syntactic rule, which says: 'In order to form one common kind of question, substitute *what* in place of an NP, and move it to the front of the sentence.'

If this solution was adopted, one would then hypothesize that the 'deep structure' of the sentences was something like (assuming Q is 'question'):

Q   *Petronella put* **what** *in the drawer*
Q   *Petronella put the parrot in* **what**

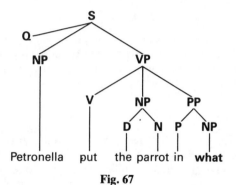

Fig. 67

A transformation would then bring *what* to the front, and the sentences would ultimately surface as:

What did Petronella put in the drawer?
What did Petronella put the parrot in?

This explanation seems even more plausible if one considers sentences containing reflexives (a word such as *himself*, *herself*), as in:

*Osbert cut **himself**.*

It is normally essential for the reflexive to be in the same clause as the person it refers to. Consider:

[Oscar said] [Osbert cut himself].

The sentence above means that Osbert cut Osbert. If Osbert had cut Oscar, the sentence would have been:

[Oscar said] [Osbert cut him].

But an important apparent exception to this rule occurs with *wh*-questions (questions beginning with *who*, *which*, *what*, and so on):

Who [did Oscar say] [—cut himself]?

The question is basically:

Who cut himself?

Yet the *who* appears to be outside the clause containing *himself*. It seems reasonable to conclude that, at some basic level, *who* and *himself* were in the same clause, perhaps something like:

[Oscar said] [Q who cut himself].

We can then assume a transformation moved *who* to the front.

Arguments such as these convince many people that sentences do indeed have two levels of structure: a deep structure and a surface structure linked by transformations.

Transformations

Let us now look more closely at the form which transformations, also known as **T-rules**, took in the (1965) Standard Theory of transformational grammar. Unlike the rewrite rules discussed in Chapter 7, each rule had *two* parts to it. First, an applicability check (usually called the **structural analysis** (SA)) which stated the structure to which the rule could be applied, and second, instructions concerning the change it brought about in this structure (called the **structural change** (SC)):

1	STRUCTURAL ANALYSIS (SA) (applicability check)
2	STRUCTURAL CHANGE (SC) (change brought about)

Fig. 68

Consider, for example, the transformation which moved adverbs to the front of a sentence, T-**adverb preposing**, as in:

Bill shrieked suddenly. ⇒ *Suddenly Bill shrieked.*

The structural analysis (applicability check) was needed in order to ensure that the sentence contained an adverb. It said (in more formal terms): 'Check that the sentence contains an adverb.' Once this had been assured, the structural change could be specified. This part of the transformation said (again in more formal terms): 'Move the adverb to the front.'

A formal way of expressing this would be to say:

SA   X – ADV
SC   X – ADV ⇒ ADV – X

Here, X is a 'variable' meaning its composition can vary. In other words, the structural analysis says: 'The sentence can contain anything you like, as long as it ends in an adverb'. The structural change says: 'X followed by an adverb changes into an adverb followed by X'.

In the Standard Theory of transformational grammar, there were maybe two dozen of these transformations, each applying to a specific structure. In addition to moving things around, as in the examples so far, others deleted items. For example, a command such as *Come!* was assumed to reflect a deeper:

IMP   *You will come.*

(where IMP stood for 'imperative'). A T-rule deleted the words *you* and *will*, and the instruction IMP. Other transformations added items. A sentence such as *There is a dodo in the garden* was assumed to reflect a more basic:

A dodo be + PRES in the garden.

A 'There-insertion' transformation added *there*.

In the sixties, confident researchers thought that sooner or later, we would compile a definitive list of all the transformations of English, and a complete specification of how they worked. Unfortunately, however, this ambitious programme was never fulfilled, for reasons which will be discussed in the next chapter.

Summary

This chapter has considered the reasons why Chomsky set up a transformational grammar in the first place, and also discussed further reasons in support of the claim that there are two levels of structure, deep structure and surface structure. It also looked in outline at the characteristics of transformations in the Standard Model of transformational grammar.

QUESTIONS

1 Define a **transformational grammar**.
2 What arguments can be put forward in favour of the claim that languages have **deep structures** as well as **surface structures**?
3 Draw an outline deep structure tree for the sentence: *What did Henry put on the table?*
4 How many parts do **T-rules** consist of, and what is the purpose of each of these?

15

Trouble with Transformations

Transformational grammar (TG) transformed linguistics, so it seemed. All linguists now had to do was to agree on the form which deep structures took, which were assumed to vary relatively little from language to language, and to produce a final and definitive list of possible transformations. At least, that was the general hope in the 1960s. However, little by little, problems crept in. Let us consider why.

Waving a magic wand

The most obvious trouble with transformations in the Standard Theory (1965) was that they appeared to be a kind of magic wand, something which could change a deep structure into any kind of surface structure by any means whatsoever. But this would clearly be absurd. We would not want a device which altered a deep structure something like:

Bill kept the dodo in the bath

into, say,

My goldfish eats bumble-bees.

There must obviously be some limits on the operations which transformations can perform. The search for the limits or **constraints** which must be placed on them has ultimately led to a fundamental reorganization of TG. In this chapter we will look at how this has happened, showing how cracks appeared in what at first looked like a magnificent theory.

Preserving the meaning

In the Standard Model of TG, the strongest constraint placed on transformations (T-rules) was that they should not be allowed to change meaning. One could therefore alter:

Bill kept a dodo in the bath.

into

A dodo was kept in the bath by Bill.
What Bill kept in the bath was a dodo.
In the bath Bill kept a dodo.

These alterations were simply stylistic nuances. They did not alter the basic proposition, that Bill kept a dodo in the bath. There was no change in the lexical items, or in who did what to whom: *Bill* remained the 'agent', the person doing the keeping, and the *dodo* was still the 'patient', the recipient of Bill's action.

This, however, was where the problems started. Certain basic transformations changed the meaning of the deep structure. The following are not the only examples of T-rules which appeared to alter meaning, but they are well-known ones.

First of all, consider **T-passive**, the T-rule which related active and passive sentences. Look at the active and passive pair:

active: *Many cowboys do not ride horses.*
passive: *Horses are not ridden by many cowboys.*

This pair, according to the Standard Theory, shared a common deep structure, so they should mean the same thing. Yet the reaction of many English speakers is that the two sentences have different interpretations. The active sentence implies that, although many cowboys do not ride horses, many still do. The passive sentence, however, suggests that hardly any cowboys ride horses.

This problem is not necessarily insoluble. One way out of the dilemma was to claim that both sentences have *two* meanings:

1   *Many cowboys do not ride horses, although many still do.*
2   *Many cowboys do not ride horses, and hardly any still do.*

The position of the word *many* in the sentence biases the interpretation of the active towards 1, and of the passive towards 2—though in theory either meaning is possible for each sentence.

But when different transformations are involved, the problems cannot be explained away so easily, as with another pair of sentences which share a common deep structure, involving a transformation known as **T-conjunction reduction**. This optionally eliminated repeated elements in sentences joined by *and*:

Few women are rich and few women are famous.
Few women are rich and famous.

In the second sentence, **T-conjunction reduction** has optionally been applied, and produced a sentence with a different meaning. If transformations do not change meaning, this should not happen.

A similar problem arose with **T-reflexive**. Once again, the following pair share a common deep structure, according to the Standard Theory:

Every candidate voted for every candidate.
Every candidate voted for himself.

Once again, most English speakers would judge the two sentences to differ in meaning. We have here yet another example of a case in which the application of a transformation has apparently resulted in a change of meaning.

These three examples show that the problem is not a trivial or isolated one. How can this dilemma be solved? One way out is to suggest that there is something odd about the sentences listed above: they all involve **quantifiers**—words such as *many*, *few*, *every*, which express a quantity. In this case, we could assume that transformations change meaning in certain circumstances, one of them being the presence of a quantifier.

This was the solution adopted by a number of linguists, who called their revised grammar the **Extended Standard Theory (EST)**, since it represented an extension of the Standard Theory, in which (as noted above) transformations could not change meaning, and the deep structure was the only input to the semantic component.

A second possible response, made by another group of linguists, was to maintain that transformations preserved meaning, but assume that the deep structure had been wrongly formulated in the first place (Figure 69). This viewpoint became known as **Generative Semantics (GS)**, for reasons which will became apparent below.

Generative semantics

The group of people who refused to accept the Extended Standard Theory (EST) claimed that the problem of T-rules which seemed to change meaning lay not so much with the T-rules themselves, as with Chomsky's conception of deep structure, which, they asserted,

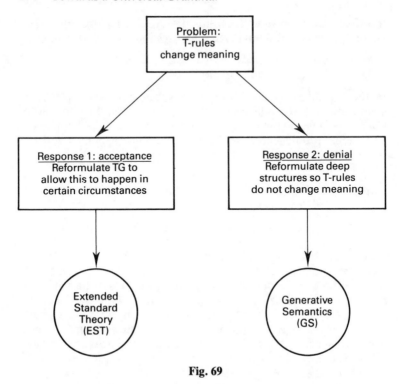

Fig. 69

was insufficiently subtle. It should be elaborated so that each member of the pairs of sentences discussed above have a different deep structure. For example, they denied that the pairs

Few women are rich and few are famous.
Few women are rich and famous.

shared a common deep structure. If these sentences had different meanings, then they *must* have different **underlying structures** (as the generative semanticists preferred to call deep structures). It was crucial for the underlying structures to deal in more detail with the 'scope' of quantifiers, the parts of the structure affected by words such as *few, many*. The main problem was to decide what these complicated and subtle underlying structures were like.

Generative semanticists, however, did not only argue that if two sentences have different meanings, they must have different underlying structures. They also argued (contrary to the Standard

Theory) that if two sentences have the same meaning, they must also have the same underlying structure. Consider the sentences:

Henry stopped Drusilla.
Henry caused Drusilla to stop.

According to the Standard Theory, the deep structures would look fairly different. The first consists of only one underlying sentence, the second of two (Figure 70).

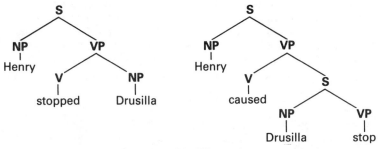

Fig. 70

According to the generative semanticists, the difference between the two sentences was purely superficial. The similarity between them could be represented if the words were decomposed into their component parts. That is, generative semanticists abandoned the assumption (made in the Standard Theory) that lexical items in the deep structure were unanalysable units. Instead, they analysed a word such as *stop* in *Henry stopped Drusilla* into CAUSE STOP, and a word such as *kill* into CAUSE DIE (or, more accurately, into CAUSE BECOME NOT ALIVE), and a word such as *remind* into STRIKE AS SIMILAR TO. Then a special type of transformation packaged up the various components into a single word.

Overall then, generative semanticists gradually elaborated their underlying structures, so much so that eventually they became indistinguishable from semantic structures. This had crucial consequences for the grammar. If underlying structures were the same as semantic structures, then clearly there was no need for them to be separate components within a grammar. The base would initiate or generate a set of underlying structures which *was* the semantic structure. For this reason, those who upheld such a theory were known as **generative semanticists**.

The general idea behind generative semantics was superficially appealing. It seemed common-sensical to many people that meanings should come first, and syntactic means of expressing them follow. Remember, however, these linguists were not talking about the processes involved in producing speech. In writing a grammar, their primary aim was to specify what was, or was not, a well-formed sentence of English. And this became increasingly difficult within the generative semantics framework.

The main problem was that of specifying the underlying structures, which became more and more unwieldy. Nobody could agree on what they should be like, and they seemed to reflect above all the intuitions of the linguists writing them, rather than any objective reality. Furthermore, they required extraordinarily complicated rules for showing how the varying sections of the underlying structure should be combined. In the end, most supporters of this approach gradually gave up on the impossible task of specifying them.

Trace theory

Eventually, the majority of TG adherents turned away from generative semantics, and admitted that at least some surface structures were important for the interpretation of meaning. Building this possibility into the grammar resulted, as mentioned above, in the **Extended Standard Theory (EST)**. As research continued, many linguists came eventually to the conclusion that the surface structure alone was responsible for meaning, and the resulting amended grammar became known as the **Revised Extended Standard Theory (REST)**.

However, the assumption that surface structures alone are responsible for meaning had several repercussions on the rest of the grammar. Above all, it became important to know where items had been moved from in the deep structure. This was necessary in order for the grammar to be able to deal with the meaning of sentences in which an NP had been shifted away from its original position, as when *what* had been switched to the front. When an NP was moved, therefore, it was assumed to leave behind a faint **trace** of its previous location, marked conventionally by the letter **t** for 'trace'. So, a deep structure something like:

*Q   Drusilla found **what** in the cave.*

would have a surface structure something like:

What *did Drusilla find **t** in the cave?* (Figure 71).

(Both the deep structure and the surface structure have been considerably simplified here, as elsewhere in this book: only the features relevant to the point under discussion are included).

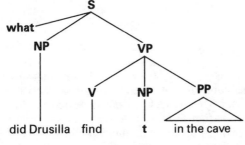

Fig. 71

Limiting the power of transformations

Since in this later version of TG (REST), the surface structures alone provided the semantic interpretation, linguists were left with the problem they started out with. How could they limit the power of transformations, and prevent them creating a hopeless morass of randomly moved items? It therefore became important to provide firm guidelines as to what could move where. One proposal was that transformations could only move items around within the structure already set up by the phrase structure rules: they could not create a totally new set of structures. In linguistic terminology, they had to be 'structure-preserving'—and a subsidiary effect of this was to alter some of the phrase structure rules.

Another proposal was to limit the distance which items could travel, so that except in exceptional circumstances, they were unable to hop too far away from their own clause. For example, take the sentence:

The discovery that the picture of the aardvark had been stolen was quite upsetting.

The phrase *of the aardvaark* was forbidden to hop outside the whole structure:

* The discovery that the picture had been stolen was quite upsetting of the aardvark.

A major preoccupation of linguists working on REST, then, was working out ways of constraining the power of transformations, in particular ways of preventing items from moving uncontrollably in all directions. But this lack of constraints was not the only problem.

Sharing out the work

A major advantage of Standard TG was that it appeared to simplify the superficial confusion of language. Instead of listing numerous sentence types, it specified a few basic patterns, and the remainder were treated as variants of these basic few.

However, in order to cope with these variants, there were literally dozens of different transformations. This large number raised its own set of problems. Above all, listing umpteen transformations which specified how to produce variants of the basic patterns was not necessarily any more economical than listing different patterns in the first place.

A further problem was that different T-rules sometimes had the same effect, yet this was not recognized in the grammar. Take the sentences:

Marigold *was impossible to please.*
Bill *seems to be ill.*

The surface structure subjects (*Marigold*, *Bill*) had been brought to the front by a transformation, the deep structure of each sentence being something like:

*It was impossible to please **Marigold**.*
*It seems that **Bill** is ill.*

Yet the transformations were quite separate, because they applied to different structures: in the first, *Marigold* is the 'object' of the verb *please*, in the second, *Bill* is the 'subject' of *is*. There was no indication in the grammar that the transformations might be linked, even though they performed similar operations.

These two problems: the large number of different transform-ations, and the fact that some of them appeared to have the same effect led people to re-examine the transformations one by one. They came to two general conclusions: first, some transformations were not 'proper' transformations, and the operations they per-formed could be dealt with better in some other component of the grammar. Second, some of the remaining transformations could be combined. Let us briefly look at the offloading and combining which took place.

Offloading

The lexicon and the semantic component were the two components which were seemingly underworked in the existing grammar, and onto which some of the existing transformations were offloaded. Consider the following sentences:

Arabella gave the champagne to Charlie.
Arabella gave Charlie the champagne.

In a Standard TG, the deep structure was somewhat like the first sentence. In order to arrive at the second, a transformation switched the words *champagne* and *Charlie*, and deleted the inter-vening *to*. But specifying this transformation turned out to be rather difficult. It certainly didn't seem to be a general rule applying to the structure V NP PP. After all, you could say:

Arabella took the picnic to the wood.
Jim donated the book to the library.
The TV station transmitted the programme to Japan.

but not

**Arabella took the wood the picnic.*
**Jim donated the library the book.*
**The TV station transmitted Japan the programme.*

In brief, this proposed transformation applies just to a few lexical items, such as *give*, *tell*, *offer*. It seems somewhat strange to have a T-rule, which is meant to be a general syntactic rule, narrowed down in this way. The lexicon might be a more obvious place for information about the structures following a few verbs. A number of 'transformations', therefore, were reassigned to the lexicon.

Other transformations were reassigned to the semantic component. For example, a Standard TG assumed that the sentence:

Antonio claimed that he was ill.

had a deep structure something like:

Antonio claimed that Antonio was ill.

Then a transformation changed the second *Antonio* to *he*. But this is a fairly unnecessary complication. A simpler alternative would be to have *he* in the deep structure to begin with, but to keep an index of NPs as they occurred, noting which ones are 'coindexed', that is, refer to the same person or thing. This would allow the semantic component to make the correct interpretation at a later stage, without any extra transformational complexities.

In general, then, the transformational component was gradually whittled down as tasks previously dealt with by transformations were offloaded onto other components in the grammar, especially the lexicon and the semantic component.

Combining

As the various transformations were peeled off, only two major processes remained: transformations which moved *wh* – (*what*, *which*, etc) around, and transformations which moved NPs around, as in:

What *did Arabella buy?*
Arabella *was difficult to please.*

which had deep structures something like:

*Q   Arabella bought **what**.*
*It was difficult to please **Arabella**.*

Yet even these two types of transformations had certain features in common, in that they both moved items to the front. Perhaps, therefore, it was suggested, there is just one basic transformation, which says: 'Items can be moved', instead of lots of different transformations, each of which had to be specified separately. This general transformation then would have to be combined with some clearly stated principles about what could be moved where.

Summary

Let us now summarize: people started with the general problem that transformations appeared to be able to do anything. Moreover, there seemed to be dozens of these powerful devices.

At first it was hoped to constrain the power of transformations by not allowing them to change meaning, but this proved to be impossible. They clearly did change meaning in a number of cases. This therefore triggered a search for new constraints, principles which would prevent them from altering sentences around in random ways.

As people sought to specify constraints, they realized that the transformations themselves were something of a ragbag, and that a number of them should be removed from the transformational component, since the task they did would be better achieved within another component of the grammar. In this way both the lexicon, and the semantic component became more important.

Transformations, meanwhile, dropped off one after the other. In the long run, only one major T-rule remained, which said in effect 'anything can be moved', but which was combined with strong constraints on what could be moved where.

These alterations paved the way for a fundamentally new version of transformational grammar, which will be the topic of the next chapter.

QUESTIONS

1   What was wrong with transformations in the Standard Theory of TG, and how did linguists hope at first to solve the problem?
2   What were the basic beliefs of **generative semanticists**, and why did they prove unsatisfactory?
3   What are **constraints**, and why are they necessary in a grammar?
4   Outline two ways in which the number of transformations was reduced.
5   What are **traces**?
6   How many major transformations eventually remained in TG?

16

The New-look Grammar

'There are three things in life you must never run after: a bus, a woman and a theory of transformational grammar: there will be another one along in a moment', commented one well-known linguist. Chomsky's new-look (1980s) grammar is radically different from the Standard Theory in a number of ways, and it is still being refined. This chapter presents a bird's-eye view of some of its main characteristics. It explains what the grammar is trying to do in general, and glosses over the intricate technical details. More information about these is contained in the works suggested for further reading at the back of the book.

Universal Grammar (UG)

Chomsky's recent model of grammar is fairly simple in its out-lines. It consists essentially of a number of different **modules** or components, each of which has a fairly specific and straightforward task to carry out. Complexities arise out of the interaction of these modules.

The framework is considered to be valid for all languages. Chomsky suggests that the basic components of **Universal Grammar (UG)** are genetically inbuilt in humans. Within various modules, there are assumed to be a number of alternative choices. One interesting speculation is that languages which are superficially quite unlike one another might be fairly similar at an underlying level. Their essential difference might be that they opted for different possible paths within a particular module—just as if, say, animals opted for air or water as their basic environment, which would in turn bring about a number of inevitable consequences. A simple decision to choose one option rather than another at a particular point would have repercussions throughout the grammar.

According to Chomsky, children automatically know what the overall options are. As they learn language, they have to find out the particular options within UG which their own language has chosen. The overall framework is inherited but, in Chomsky's words, it is used in connection with 'parameters that have to be fixed by experience'. In other words, the particular value which a language has decided upon at the option points have to be discovered afresh by each child who learns the language. There may be very few actual choices to be made, though these would have far-reaching consequences.

The possible option points are still speculative, though some suggestions have been made. For example, within phrases, one possible choice might be between having the **head** (main word) at the beginning of a phrase (as in the English PP *up the tree*) or at the end (as in Turkish, which says, as it were, *the tree up*). This would have far-reaching effects on the form of sentences. For example, an English sentence such as:

The man who fell downstairs broke his leg.

would, in a language such as Turkish, turn out to have a literal translation something like:

The downstairs-fell man his leg broke.

Pro-drop might be another crucial option. That is, there might be an important division between languages which allow their speakers to drop the pronouns at the beginning of a sentence, and those which do not. For example, Italian is a pro-drop language. It is possible to say either:

Sono Inglese.	or	*Io sono Inglese.*
'Am English'		'I am English'

In English, only the second option, the one with the pronoun, is possible. The path taken would have repercussions throughout the grammar, some of them unexpected ones. For example, consider the English sentence:

Angela thought that Hezekiah was stupid.

This has a corresponding question:

Who did Angela think was stupid?

For some strange reason, the word *that* has to be omitted in the question. You cannot say:

★Who did Angela think that was stupid?

This odd fact seems to be characteristic of non-pro-drop languages. Pro-drop languages such as Italian seem able to leave the *that* in.

In the long run, linguists hope to specify all of the crucial option points, and their repercussions. These then would have to be built into the overall framework. If this is ever achieved, then linguists will have gone a long way towards achieving their ultimate goal of specifying UG. So far, however, most of this is a hope for the future, and linguists are still trying to sort out the overall arrangement of modules within the grammar.

From deep structure to D-structure

Superficially, the most obvious difference between the new type TG and the Standard one is the renaming of some of the essential ingredients, so as not to confuse them with the old ones. Deep structure in its altered form has been relabelled **D-structure**, and the revised surface structure has been relabelled **S-structure**. The old semantic representation has been superseded by **LF** 'logical form', and the phonetic representation is now labelled **PF** 'phonetic form' (Figure 72).

Fig. 72

These levels are linked by processes which have certain superficial resemblances to the older-style TG: PS rules specify the D-structure. D-structure and S-structure are linked by transformational operations, though (as discussed in the previous chapter), the transformational component is a mere shadow of its former self. PF rules convert the S-structure into PF, and LF rules convert the S-structure into LF (Figure 73).

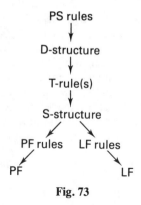

Fig. 73

However, not one of these levels is truly similar to the comparable level in an old style TG, nor are the rules which operate on them the same. For example, the LF rules and LF contain a considerable amount of material which belonged strictly to the syntax in a Standard TG. Furthermore, as will become clear, there are a number of additional modules containing sets of principles which apply to the various levels.

Government and binding

The new-look grammar was presented by Chomsky in a series of lectures published under the title: *Lectures on government and binding* (1981). The name has stuck. It is usually referred to as **government-binding theory**, or **GB**. Before going on to look at the various modules which go to make up the grammar, let us consider why it has been given this name.

This somewhat strange label is because GB pays particular attention to two aspects of grammar which were virtually ignored in the Standard Theory, **government** on the one hand, and **binding** on the other. Government involves the notion of a constituent having power over others, and binding deals with the linking or binding of items to one another. Let us briefly outline what each involves.

The general notion of government has been around in linguistics for a long time, in that it has long been recognized that some words have influence over, or govern other words. For example, in Latin grammars grammarians spoke of prepositions governing nouns, since a preposition such as *contra* 'against', as in 'fight against the

Gauls' caused the following word, *Gauls*, to have a particular ending. In the more recent (somewhat altered) usage, the word **government** is usually used in connection with heads of phrases which influence others in their immediate locality, in the sense of requiring them to exist as subsidiaries to themselves. For example, in English, a verb such as *hit* governs a following NP, as in *hit the donkey*, and a preposition such as *up* also governs an NP, as in *up the tree*. The nodes involved are normally sisters, daughters of the same mother (Chapter 7).

Fig. 74

However, quite often there is an important relationship between words which are on different branches and on different levels, as in the sentence:

Drusilla had a dream about herself (Figure 75).

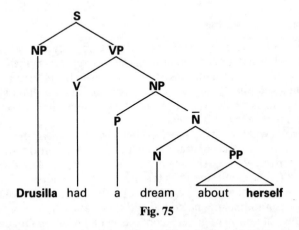

Fig. 75

Drusilla and *herself* are on different branches, and different levels, yet clearly they have an intimate relationship, which needs to be carefully specified, since one could not randomly alter it around. It is impossible to say, for example:

*Herself had a dream about Drusilla.
*Drusilla had a dream about Peter kissing herself.

Furthermore, it is important to understand the relationship in order to interpret sentences properly. Consider the sentences:

Henry read the report about Toby stabbing himself.
Henry read the report about Toby stabbing him.

It is essential to realize that Toby was stabbed in the first sentence, but Henry (or someone else) in the second.

A major part of Chomsky's new theory is to try and specify exactly which parts of trees influence one another, and which can be linked in their interpretation. He and his followers have tried to draw up a wider notion of government, known as **command**. A principle known as **c-command** (from 'constituent command') specifies which constituents have power over others in a total tree structure. There is some dispute about exactly how to phrase c-command, but in general, (and somewhat simplified), it says that when a node branches, items on the first branch have some influence over those on the second branch, irrespective of how high or low on the tree they come. So, in Figure 75, the first NP *Drusilla* c-commands the VP, and every node under it. The main verb *had* c-commands the NP following, and every node under it, and so on.

The notion of c-command enables one to specify relationships and restrictions between different parts of the sentence. For example, one could say that the word *herself* in the sentence above must be c-commanded by the person referred to. This would preclude impossible sentences such as:

*Herself had a dream about Drusilla.

Furthermore, the notion could be used with other constructions, such as:

The politicians argued with one another.

One could specify that a phrase such as *one another* must be c-commanded by the phrase it refers back to, so precluding:

*Each other argued with the politicians.

More generally, one could say that words which refer back to others, traditionally known as **anaphors**, have to be c-commanded by the words they refer back to, their **antecedents**. Therefore, a general structural relationship, that of c-command could enable one to specify quite simply a large number of apparently separate restrictions, which would have had to be stated one by one in an old style transformational grammar.

Binding is strongly interlinked with the notion of c-command. Briefly, a **binding principle** states that when two NPs are **co-indexed**—refer to the same thing or person, as with *Marigold* and *herself* in *Marigold cut herself*—then the antecedent (*Marigold*) must c-command the anaphor (*herself*). If so, it has been **properly bound**: in other words, there is a proper link between the two NPs. In contrast, a sequence such as:

★Herself cut Marigold.

would be impossible, because *herself* was not properly bound. Binding relates above all to the interpretation of sentences, since it shows which items are to be interpreted as linked together.

All this may seem somewhat like common sense, given these simple examples, and it looks at first sight as if one could just rephrase all this by saying antecedents come before anaphors. But the necessity of specifying a structural relationship between NPs becomes apparent as sentences get more complex, as in:

*Who did Marigold claim cut **herself**?*

The surface structure of this sentence would be something like:

*Who did Marigold claim **t** cut **herself**.*

We need fairly detailed mechanisms to specify the linking of *herself* and *t*, and *t* and *who*, so allowing one to interpret *who* and *herself* together, rather than *Marigold* and *herself*.

To summarize so far, the government and binding approach is particularly concerned about relationships between constituents. It specifies which constituents have power over others, the overall purpose being to express simply and clearly which nodes on a tree are interlinked. Only certain links are possible, and discovering and describing these enables us to grasp the principles underlying sentence interpretation.

This type of grammar shows, moreover, a shift of perspective. In the early years of TG, a grammar was essentially a device which specified what was, and what was not, a well-formed sentence. In this recent version, emphasis has been moved to a specification of the general principles and relationships which exist within language.

Multiple modules

Let us now look in outline at the various modules which constitute a GB model of grammar (Figure 76).

Starting at the top of the diagram, the grammar first contains phrase-structure rules formulated in accordance with **X-bar theory** (Chapter 7). These specify the tree-structures in the D-structure. The lexicon feeds into this D-structure.

At this level, one further set of principles applies, known as **theta-theory** or θ**-theory**. This is short for 'thematic relations theory', which deals with who does what to whom by specifying the roles played by NPs, such as **agent** (the NP which does the actions) and **patient** or **theme** (the NP which undergoes the action of the verb):

agent		**patient or theme**
Albert	ate	*spaghetti.*

θ-theory is perhaps the most widely applicable module, since it affects the D-structure, the lexicon (the θ-roles attached to each verb are specified there), the S-structure and the LF (where the θ-roles of the traces are taken into consideration).

Moving down the page, one next comes to the single remaining **transformation** 'Move α'. α is known as a 'variable', which simply means that it can stand for anything. In effect, therefore the transformation says: 'Move anything'. But this apparent licence for anything to happen is illusory, since quite severe restrictions cut down on the movements which can take place. In particular, constituents can be moved only in smallish hops, within certain bounds, so that this part of the total mechanism is known as **bounding theory** (not to be confused with **binding theory**, which links constituents together).

Arriving at S-structure, there is now a component known as **case-theory** through which a 'case' is assigned to every NP, via a 'case-assigner'. In English, the main case-assigners are verbs. For example, a verb with a tense ending (usually referred to as INFL) assigns its subject the case 'nominative', and its object the case 'accusative', as in the sentence:

Marigold	*hit + INFL*	*Fred*
nominative	← **case assigner** →	**accusative**

This section of the grammar is somewhat more important than appears at first sight. For example, at D-level, a passive sentence might appear as something like:

—*be + INFL shot Paul*

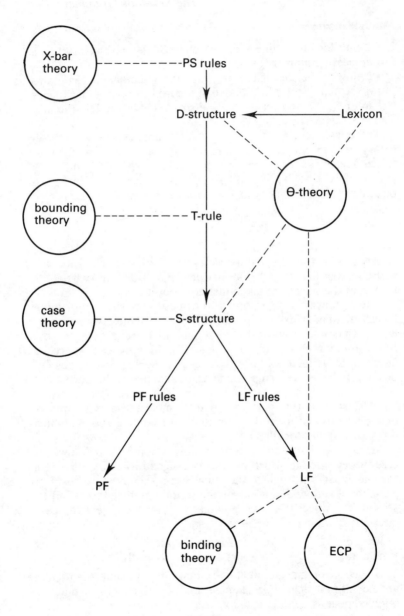

Fig. 76

The 'gap' at the beginning of the sentence is clearly not permitted as a final result, as we cannot say:

★Was shot Paul.

Since a verb + INFL has to have a nominative subject, it assigns it to *Paul*, which is dragged round to the front of the sentence, eventually resulting in:

Paul was shot.

However, this module is in a state of flux at the moment, since Chomsky (and others) have suggested that it might be eventually be integrated into θ-theory.

Between the S-structure and the PF (phonetic form) there are various PF rules specifying how to change the S-structure into the PF, and, similarly, between the S-structure and the LF (logical form) there are various LF rules for dealing with the relationship between the surface order and the meaning of the sentence.

Two important modules affect the LF. **Binding theory** specifies how anaphors and their antecedents are to be recognized and interpreted (as discussed earlier in the chapter). The **Empty Category Principle (ECP)** specifies how to deal with apparent gaps in the structure in cases where items do not appear. For example, consider the sentences:

Aloysius wants Pamela to go.
Aloysius wants—to go.

In the second sentence, the person who is to go is not overtly specified, yet native speakers know that it is Aloysius. Therefore the grammar requires a principle showing how this interpretation is reached.

This is the general set-up of GB, according to majority opinion. However, it is being amended and revised continuously, and there is considerable controversy over the details. In ten years time, it might look quite different, or even have been abandoned.

Furthermore, it is not clear that Chomsky's GB model is necessarily the best for human language. There have been several other proposed, and at least two are being explored by a large number of linguists: first, there is a model which dispenses with transformations altogether, and has far more sophisticated phrase structure rules instead, a so-called **generalized phrase structure grammar** (GPSG). This has been proposed by the British linguist Gerald Gazdar. Second, there is a model which gives much greater prominence to the lexicon, a so-called **lexical functional grammar**. This is associated with an American scholar, Joan Bresnan. Some of the works recommended for further reading on p. 195 provide information about these. Only time will tell whether either of these models will prove more satisfactory than GB, or whether some entirely new model will take its place. Meanwhile, Chomsky's model at present has more adherents than either of the other two, which is why it has been given prominence in this book.

QUESTIONS

1   What do the terms **D-structure**, **S-structure**, **LF** and **PF** mean, and how are they organized in relation to one another in Chomsky's recent model of grammar?
2   What do the terms **government** and **c-command** mean?
3   What is θ**-theory**, and which parts of a grammar does it affect?
4   Distinguish between **binding** and **bounding theory**.

Suggestions for Further Reading

General background

Akmajian, A., Demers, R. A., and Harnish, R. M. *Linguistics: An introduction to language and communication*, 2nd edition (Cambridge, MA: MIT Press, 1984).
A wide-ranging and easy to read introductory course.

Atkinson, M., Kilby, D. and Roca, I. *Foundations of general linguistics* (London: Allen and Unwin, 1982).
A clear and reliable introduction to the main areas of linguistics.

Clark, V. P., Escholz, P. A. and Rosa, A. F. *Language: Introductory readings*, 4th edition (New York: St. Martin's Press, 1985).
A range of readable readings on different topics within linguistics.

Fromkin, V. and Rodman, R. *An introduction to language*, 3rd edition (New York: Holt, Rinehart and Winston, 1983).
Another broad-ranging and readable introductory course.

Graddol, D., Cheshire, J., and Swann, J., *Describing Language* (Milton Keynes: Open University Press, 1987).
A straightforward introduction with useful sections on the analysis of conversation and texts.

Hudson, R. *Invitation to linguistics* (Oxford: Martin Robertson, 1984).
An introductory book which gets across what it's like to 'do' linguistics.

Lyons, J. *Language and linguistics* (Cambridge: Cambridge University Press, 1981).
An intelligent outline of some basic theoretical notions.

Palmer, F. *Grammar*, 2nd edition. (Harmondsworth, Middx.: Penguin, 1983).
A useful discussion of how traditional grammatical concepts tie in with modern linguistics.

Smith, N. and Wilson, D. *Modern linguistics: The results of Chomsky's revolution* (Harmondsworth, Middx: Penguin, 1979).
A summary and assessment of Chomsky's earlier ideas.

Yule, G. *The study of language* (Cambridge: Cambridge University Press, 1985).
An outline survey.

Recent history of linguistics

Anderson, S. R. *Phonology in the twentieth century* (Chicago: University of Chicago Press, 1985).
Ways in which sound patterns have been analysed this century.

Newmeyer, F. J. *Linguistic theory in America* (New York: Academic Press, 1980).
An account of the first quarter century of transformational grammar.

Sampson, G. *Schools of linguistics* (London: Hutchinson, 1980).
A readable survey relating fashions in linguistics to general intellectual trends over the past two centuries.

Phonetics and phonology

Gimson, A. C. *An introduction to the pronunciation of English*, 3rd edition. (London: Arnold 1980).
The standard guide to the sounds of British English.

Hawkins, P. *Introducing phonology* (London: Hutchinson, 1984).
A useful introduction, though requires an outline knowledge of phonetics.

Hogg, R. and McCully, C. B. *Metrical phonology: a coursebook* (Cambridge: Cambridge University Press, 1987).
A clear introduction to important recent developments in phonological theory.

Lass, R. *Phonology* (Cambridge: Cambridge University Press, 1984).
An intermediate level book.

Ladefoged, P. *A course in phonetics*, 2nd edition. (New York: Harcourt Brace Jovanovich, 1982).
A broad general introduction, covering sounds from a wide variety of languages.

Roach, P. *English phonetics and phonology* (Cambridge: Cambridge University Press, 1983).
A clear and straightforward account for beginners.

Wells, J. C. *Accents of English*, vols. 1–3. (Cambridge: Cambridge University Press, 1982).
A survey of the various types of English accent found both in England and around the world.

Syntax

Brown, E. K. *Linguistics today* (London: Fontana, 1984).
A clear exposition of some basic principles which underlie the linguistic analysis of sentence structure.

Chomsky, N. *Knowledge of language: its nature, origin and use* (New York: Praeger, 1985).
Chomsky's most recent semi-technical account of his ideas.

Radford, A. *Transformational syntax* (Cambridge: Cambridge University Press, 1981).
An introduction to transformational grammar (REST version).

Sells, P. *Lectures on contemporary syntactic theories* (Stanford, CA: Stanford University Center for the Study of Language and Information, 1985).
A brief outline account of TG (GB version), generalized phrase structure grammar, and lexical-functional grammar.

Van Riemsdijk, H. and Williams, E. *Introduction to the theory of grammar* (Cambridge, MA: MIT Press, 1986).
An up-to-date introduction to recent models of TG.

Wekker, H. and Haegeman, L. *A modern course in English syntax* (London: Croom Helm, 1985).
An intermediate level course, which aims at equipping people both with a knowledge of English syntax, and a relatively recent version of TG (REST).

Semantics and pragmatics

Allan, K. *Linguistic meaning*, vols. 1–2. (London: Routledge & Kegan Paul, 1986).
A broad survey which covers both semantics (vol. 1) and pragmatics (vol. 2).

Brown, G. and Yule, G. *Discourse analysis* (Cambridge: Cambridge University Press, 1983).
A clear outline survey of a confusing topic.

Hurford, J. and Heasley, B. *Semantics: a coursebook* (Cambridge: Cambridge University Press, 1983).
A helpful book which explains semantic concepts by means of practical exercises.

Leech, G. *Principles of pragmatics* (London: Longman, 1983).
An analysis of the goals of language, and an account of various theories which have tried to tackle this topic.

Lyons, G. *Language, meaning and context* (London: Fontana, 1981).
A sensible survey of the field.

Stubbs, M. *Discourse analysis* (Oxford: Basil Blackwell, 1983).
A book which surveys various approaches to discourse analysis.

Wardaugh, R. *How conversation works* (Oxford: Basil Blackwell, 1985).
A readable book which spans the area between pragmatics and sociolinguistics.

Sociolinguistics

Coates, J. *Women, men and language* (London: Longman, 1986).
An exceptionally clear account of research on language and sex.

Downes, W. D. *Language and society* (London: Fontana, 1984).
A survey which covers language variation caused by social background and social situation, with good discussions of problem areas.

Milroy, L. *Language and social networks*, 2nd edition. (Oxford: Basil Blackwell, 1986).
A pioneering sociolinguistic study.

Mühlhäusler, P. *Pidgin and creole linguistics* (Oxford: Basil Blackwell, 1986).
An authoritative account of pidginization and creolization.

Todd, L. *Modern Englishes: Pidgins and creoles* (Oxford: Basil Blackwell, 1984).
A useful introductory survey of pidgins and creoles.

Trudgill, P. *Sociolinguistics*, 2nd edition. (Harmondsworth, Middx.: Penguin, 1983).
A highly readable and reliable brief introduction to language variation.

Wardaugh, R. *An introduction to sociolinguistics* (Oxford: Basil Blackwell, 1986).
A clear and comprehensive outline survey.

Psycholinguistics

Aitchison, J. *The articulate mammal: An introduction to psycholinguistics*, 2nd edition (London: Hutchinson, 1983; New York: Universe).
An easy to read introduction.

Aitchison, J. *Words in the mind: An introduction to the mental lexicon* (Oxford: Basil Blackwell, 1987).
A readable account of how people store and find lexical items.

Ellis, A. and Beattie, G. *The psychology of language and communication* (London: Weidenfeld & Nicolson, 1986).
A broad survey of the psychology of communication.

Fletcher, P. and Garman, M. *Language acquisition*, 2nd edition. (Cambridge: Cambridge University Press, 1986).
A survey of various areas within child language written by experts.

Garnham, A. *Psycholinguistics: Central topics* (London: Methuen, 1985).
A useful overview, written by a psychologist.

Matthei, E. and Roeper, T. *Understanding and producing speech* (London: Fontana, 1983; New York: Universe).
A brief and useful introduction.

Wanner, E. and Gleitman, L. R. *Language acquisition: The state of the art* (Cambridge: Cambridge University Press, 1982).
Another useful survey.

Historical linguistics and typology
Aitchison, J. *Language change: Progress or decay?* (London: Fontana, 1981; New York: Universe).
A readable introduction to how and why language changes.

Bynon, T. *Historical linguistics* (Cambridge: Cambridge University Press, 1977).
An account of the main theories which have influenced the study of language change over the past century.

Comrie, B. *Language universals and linguistic typology* (Oxford: Basil Blackwell, 1981).
A clear and useful survey of attempts to divide languages up into different types.

Shopen, T. *Language typology and syntactic description*, vols. 1–3 (Cambridge: Cambridge University Press, 1985).
Three volumes which attempt to provide an overview of structures found in the languages of the world.

Computational linguistics
Grishman, R. *Computational linguistics: an introduction* (Cambridge: Cambridge University Press, 1986).
An overview of recent approaches to the computer analysis of language.

Applied linguistics
Klein, W. *Second language acquisition* (Cambridge: Cambridge University Press, 1986).
An outline account of some theoretical and practical issues.

Writing
Sampson, G. *Writing systems* (London: Hutchinson, 1985)
A clear survey of writing systems.

List of Symbols and Main Abbreviations

(Phonetic symbols used are listed on p. 48).

[ ]	used for phonetic transcription
/ /	used for phonemic transcription
( )	denotes an optional item
$\left\{ \begin{matrix} X \\ Y \end{matrix} \right\}$	indicates alternatives, 'either X or Y'.
★	indicates an ill-formed sentence or word
→	means 'rewrite as'
ø	means 'zero'
#	indicates a word boundary
/	means 'in the environment of'
	e.g. [l] → [ł]/—# means rewrite [l] as [ł] before a word boundary (i.e. at the end of a word)
S	sentence
N	Noun
NP	Noun phrase
V	Verb
VP	Verb phrase
A	Adjective
AP	Adjective phrase
P	Preposition
PP	Preposition phrase

Index

Index

accent and dialect, 106
acquisition of language, *see* child
    language
adjacency pairs, *see* exchanges
agglutinating languages, 149
allomorphs, 62–4
allophones, 48–50
analogy, 136–7
analytical languages, *see* isolating
    languages
anaphora, 187–8
animal communication, 19–26, 122
anthropological linguistics, 15, 17
antonyms, *see* opposites
applied linguistics, 15, 17, 142–3
arbitrary symbols, 20
areal features, 148
artificial intelligence (AI), 15, 101
assemblage errors, 127

binding, *see* government and
    binding
Bloomfield, Leonard, 32–3, 56

caregiver language, 121–2
C-command, 187–8
chain shifts, 137–8
change, *see* language change
child language, 120–4
Chomsky, Noam, 33–5, 157–92
classification (inclusion), 91

comparative grammar, 30 *see also*
    comparative historical
    linguistics, contrastive
    linguistics
comparative historical linguistics,
    139, 143–7
comparative philology, 139
complex sentences, 80–83
componential analysis, 87–8
comprehension, 124–5
computational linguistics, 15, 17
configurational languages, 68, 150
conjoining, 81
consonants, English, 48
constituent analysis, 69–75
constraints, 34, 157, 171, 177–8
content-process controversy, 121–2
contrastive linguistics, 142–3
conversational analysis, 103–4
    implicatures, 98–9
    maxims, 98–9
cooperative principle, 98–9
count and mass nouns, 40
creativity, 22, 34
creoles, 117
cultural transmission, 21

Darwin, Charles, 30
decomposition of lexical items,
    87–8
decreolization, 117
deep structure, 161–8

derivational morphemes, 62
descriptive grammars, 31–2
descriptive and prescriptive
    approach, 12–13
diachronic linguistics, 18 *see also*
    language change
dialect, 106
diphthongs, 48
discourse analysis, 97, 101–3
discovery procedures, 33
displacement, 22
distinctive features, 51–2
domination, 71
double articulation, *see* duality
drum messages, *see* talking drums
duality, 21–2

embedding, 81–3
entailment, 93–4
exchanges, 103
explicitness, 34, 73
Extended Standard Theory (EST),
    173–4
external reconstruction, 139, 143–7

family resemblances, 91–3
family tree, 146
features (of phonemes), 51–2
felicity conditions, *see* happiness
    conditions
foot, 54
form and substance, 16
frames, 101
free and bound morphemes, 61
free variation, 49
functions of language, 27, 36
function words, 69
fusional languages, 150
fuzziness, 91–3

game, language like a, 16, 24, 31,
    36–7
Genie, 121
generative grammars, 34, 157
generative semantics, 173–6

government and binding (GB),
    185–92
grammar,
    comparative, *see* comparative
        grammar
    components of, 16, 38
    definition of, 16, 34, 38
    descriptive, *see* descriptive
        grammars
    generative, *see* generative
        grammars
    phrase structure, *see* phrase
        structure grammars
    traditional, *see* traditional
        grammars
    transformational, *see*
        transformational grammars
    universal, *see* universal grammar
Grice, Paul, 98

happiness conditions, 100
head (of phrase), 80, 152, 183
historical linguistics, 17–18
    see also language change, sound
        change
history of linguistics, 29–35
homonyms, 59
hyponyms, 91

implicational universals, 140, 149
inclusion, 91
Indo-European, 30–31 *see also*
    Proto-Indo-European
inflection and derivation, 61–2
inflections, 69
innateness, 21, 120–1
internal reconstruction, 139
International Phonetic Alphabet
    (IPA), 45–8
isolating languages, 149

Jones, Sir William, 30

Labov, William, 110, 132–3
language change, 30–1, 131–41

language, characteristics of, 19–27, 105
   functions of, 27, 36
   origin of, 27
   types, 148–53
   universals, 33–4, 38–40, 157–92
   variation, 105–118
lexical diffusion, 134
lexical-functional grammar, 192
lexical sets, 87–8
lexicon, 77–9
lingua franca, 116
linguistics, definition of, 11–15
   history of, 29–35
   scope of, 15–18
logic, formal, 91, 93–4

maturationally controlled behaviour, 120–1
meaning, 15–16, 85–94, 124
metrical phonology, 53–4
Milroy, Leslie, 113
minimal pairs, 47
Montague semantics, 94
morphemes, 60–4
morphology, 16, 60–4
morphophonology, 62–3
motherese, *see* caregiver language
multilingual communities, 115

natural class (of sounds), 52
natural tendencies, 135–6
non-segmental phonemes, 52–3
NP tests, 75

opposites, 89–90
overgeneralization, 122–4

parallel processing, 125
parameters, 183
parts of speech, *see* word classes
perceptual strategies, 125–6
philosophical linguistics, 15, 17
phonemes, 21, 47–55
phonetics, 15–16, 45–6
phonology, 15–16

phrase structure grammars, 159
pidgins, 116–7
power and solidarity, 108–9
pragmatics, 15, 17, 97–104
prescriptive and descriptive approach, 12–13
pro-drop languages, 151, 183
production (of speech), 126–8
productivity, *see* creativity
Proto-Indo-European, 30–1, 146–7
prototypes, 92–3, 124
psycholinguistics, 15, 17, 118–28
psychology of communication, 19, 118
pure vowels and diphthongs, 48

Received Pronunciation (RP), 47
reconstruction, 139–41, 143–7
recursion, 82–3
registers, 106–8
Revised Extended Standard Theory (REST), 176–81
rewrite rules, 71–3, 76–9, 82

Sapir, Edward, 150
Saussure, Ferdinand de, 16, 31
selection errors, 127
semantics, 15–16, *see also* meaning
serial and parallel processing, 125
sex differences, 114–15
slips of the tongue, 126–8
social class differences, 109–12
social networks, 113
sociolinguistics, 15, 17, 105–18
sound change, 30–1, 131–8
sounds, use of, 19–20, 21 *see also* phonemes, phonetics, phonology
speech acts, 99–101
speech community, 105–6
spoken and written language, 13–14
spreading activation, 125
structuralists, 32–3
structural linguistics, 31–2
structure dependence, 24–6

stylistics, 15, 17, 102
substance and form, 16
surface and deep structure, 161–8
synchronic and diachronic
      linguistics, 18
synonyms, 89–90
syntactic change, 138–9
syntactic devices, 68–9
syntax, 15–16, 68–83

talking drums, 52–3
therapeutic change, 136–8
'tip of the tongue' experiment,
      127–8
tone languages, 52–3
traditional grammar, 12–15
traces, 176–7, 188
transformational grammar (TG),
      32, 157–92
transformations, 163, 168–9,
      171–81, 189–90
tree diagrams, 53–4, 70–1, 79–80
tree, family, *see* family tree

turn-taking, 37, 103
typological reconstruction, 139–40
typology, 18, 148–53, 182–4

universal grammar, 15, 33–4,
      38–40, 157–92
variation in language, 105–18
vowels, English, 48

word classes, 65–7
      order, 68, 150–3
      recognition, 124–5
      selection, 126–8
      types and tokens, 57
words, definition of, 56–8
      identification of, 59–60
written and spoken language,
      13–14, 45

X-bar syntax, 79–80, 189–90

Young Grammarians, 30–1